EVOLVE

WORKBOOK

Mari Vargo

6

CAMBRIDGE
UNIVERSITY PRESS

CAMBRIDGE
UNIVERSITY PRESS

University Printing House, Cambridge CB2 8BS, United Kingdom

One Liberty Plaza, 20th Floor, New York, NY 10006, USA

477 Williamstown Road, Port Melbourne, VIC 3207, Australia

314–321, 3rd Floor, Plot 3, Splendor Forum, Jasola District Centre, New Delhi – 110025, India

103 Penang Road, #05-06/07, Visioncrest Commercial, Singapore 238467

Cambridge University Press is part of the University of Cambridge.

It furthers the University's mission by disseminating knowledge in the pursuit of education, learning and research at the highest international levels of excellence.

www.cambridge.org
Information on this title: www.cambridge.org/9781108409094

© Cambridge University Press 2020

First published 2020

20 19 18 17 16 15 14 13 12 11 10 9 8

Printed in Great Britain by CPI Group (UK) Ltd, Croydon CR0 4YY

A catalogue record for this publication is available from the British Library

ISBN 978-1-108-40535-5 Student's Book
ISBN 978-1-108-40514-0 Student's Book A
ISBN 978-1-108-40931-5 Student's Book B
ISBN 978-1-108-40537-9 Student's Book with Practice Extra
ISBN 978-1-108-40515-7 Student's Book with Practice Extra A
ISBN 978-1-108-40932-2 Student's Book with Practice Extra B
ISBN 978-1-108-40909-4 Workbook with Audio
ISBN 978-1-108-40885-1 Workbook with Audio A
ISBN 978-1-108-41196-7 Workbook with Audio B
ISBN 978-1-108-40520-1 Teacher's Edition with Test Generator
ISBN 978-1-108-41077-9 Presentation Plus
ISBN 978-1-108-41206-3 Class Audio CDs
ISBN 978-1-108-40802-8 Video Resource Book with DVD
ISBN 978-1-108-41451-7 Full Contact with DVD
ISBN 978-1-108-41157-8 Full Contact with DVD A
ISBN 978-1-108-41424-1 Full Contact with DVD B

Additional resources for this publication at www.cambridge.org/evolve

CONTENTS

1.1 THE ROBOT TOUCH

1 VOCABULARY: Using adverbs to add detail

A **Match the adverbs with the definitions.**

1	comprehensively	_c_	**a**	certain to happen
2	ultimately		**b**	definitely
3	demonstrably		**c**	in a complete way
4	inevitably		**d**	little by little; in a gradual way
5	drastically		**e**	in the end
6	progressively		**f**	in a reasonable way
7	undoubtedly		**g**	in a way that can be shown or proven
8	feasibly		**h**	in an extreme way

B **Find the words.**

~~dramatically~~   gradually   increasingly   markedly   potentially   radically   unquestionably

R	A	T	P	O	K	G	F	D	C	U	I	A	P	R	C
E	K	S	O	J	E	S	M	V	T	K	X	N	N	A	P
U	N	Q	U	E	S	T	I	O	N	A	B	L	Y	D	O
T	R	Y	G	H	G	K	Q	U	S	I	E	Q	P	I	T
P	N	I	L	Y	R	C	P	N	H	N	L	L	Y	C	E
I	N	C	R	E	A	S	I	N	G	L	Y	G	K	A	N
L	Y	M	S	M	D	G	L	D	I	C	R	A	J	L	T
Y	K	T	S	M	U	U	Y	V	N	M	P	E	S	L	I
C	G	M	D	R	A	M	A	T	I	C	A	L	L	Y	A
I	R	L	L	Y	L	R	I	F	L	H	K	O	T	B	L
E	K	I	O	T	L	K	D	U	Y	C	R	L	L	Y	L
G	P	S	D	N	Y	C	Z	M	A	R	K	E	D	L	Y

2 GRAMMAR: Commenting adverbs with future forms

A **Put the words in the correct order to make sentences.**

1 part / lives in / robots will / of our / a big / inevitably / be / the future / .

Robots will inevitably be a big part of our lives in the future.

2 many / potentially / they are / types / take over / different / going to / of jobs / .

3 able / some / certainly / not be / jobs / they will / to do / .

4 progressively / more dependent / on robots / however, we / become / will / .

3 | GRAMMAR AND VOCABULARY

A **Write sentences about the future using the word prompts and a commenting adverb.**

1 Some people believe / robots / look more human

   Some people believe robots will gradually look more human.

2 They / move and talk more like us

3 Robots / become involved in our personal lives

4 According to some people, we / develop relationships with robots

5 We / have robots as our friends and coworkers

6 Robots / make our lives easier.

7 Having robots around / improve our quality of life.

8 It / be impossible to tell the difference between robots and humans

B **How do you think life will be different with robots? Complete the sentences with the commenting adverbs in parentheses and your own ideas.**

1 Every home (ultimately)

2 Robots (increasingly)

3 Hospitals (potentially)

4 Robots (drastically)

5 Cities (inevitably)

1 VOCABULARY: Talking about developments in technology

A Complete the conversations with words from the boxes.

Conversation 1

> artificial intelligence   beta version   chatbots
> facial recognition   virtual assistants   voice activation
> working prototype

Pia   What are you reading, Sam?

Sam   I'm reading an article about AI.

Pia   What's AI?

Sam   It stands for [1] _artificial intelligence_ . This company is developing [2] _____ to talk to their customers online. So far, they have developed a [3] _____ . This early version still has a lot of problems. They think their [4] _____ will be ready in a couple of years.

Pia   That's interesting. Are they only going to use it for customer service?

Sam   Well, right now the company is using simpler chatbots as [5] _____ . These devices use [6] _____ , so you just talk to them to turn them on. They also have cameras and use [7] _____ , so when you look at them, they know who you are.

Conversation 2

> computer-generated speech   computer translation   image recognition
> operating system   text to speech   voice recognition

Carlo   Hey, Allie, what are you doing?

Allie   I'm getting ready for my trip to Italy. I'm downloading a new app. It's a [8] _____ app because I don't speak much Italian.

Carlo   Cool. Is it easy to use?

Allie   It's really easy to use. You just say something in English. The computer uses [9] _____ , so it understands what you say and shows you the Italian translation. It also uses [10] _____ , so your phone can say the words after translating them.

Carlo   That's cool. Does it sound like a real person, or does it sound like really bad [11] _____ ?

Allie   It sounds like a real person. It uses [12] _____ , too, so you can take a photo of text and the phone can translate the text from the picture.

Carlo   I could really use that. I wonder if it would work with my [13] _____ .

Allie   It should work on any phone or tablet. You should try it!

2 GRAMMAR: Future perfect and future continuous

A **Find the errors and rewrite each sentence.**

1 I'll staying at my sister's house next week.

2 We'll have finish dinner before the movie starts.

3 I have taken eight classes by the end of the year.

4 You be working with Kim on this project.

5 Everyone will leave by the time Mark gets here.

B (Circle) **the correct phrases to complete the conversation.**

Pedro Are you excited about your trip?

Yuki Yes, I am! Tomorrow morning, ¹(*I'll be driving*)/ *I'll have driven* to my friend Tina's house by the beach.

Pedro Have you been there before?

Yuki No, I haven't, so ²*I'll be using / I'll have used the* GPS to find her house.

Pedro ³*Will you be studying / Will you have studied* while you're there?

Yuki No, ⁴*I'll be finishing / I'll have finished* all my schoolwork, so ⁵*I'll be relaxing / I'll have relaxed* on the beach.

Pedro Is anyone else going to be there with you?

Yuki Yes, our friend Sarah is also coming. She's leaving tonight, so ⁶*she'll be arriving / she'll have arrived* by the time I get there.

Pedro ⁷*How long will you be staying / How long will you have stayed*?

Yuki I'll be there for a week. I can't wait! ⁸*We'll be talking and having fun / We'll have talked and had fun* all week long.

3 GRAMMAR AND VOCABULARY

A **Answer the questions with your own ideas about developments in technology. Write complete sentences.**

1 In twenty years, what new technology do you think will be available that we don't have now?

2 What technology will have disappeared?

3 What technology will we be using all the time?

4 What things will we still be able to do without technology?

I GET WHAT YOU'RE SAYING ...

1 LISTENING

A 🔊 **1.01** **LISTEN FOR ATTITUDE** Listen to a conversation between two friends, Carrie and Paul. Answer the questions.

1 Does Carrie like the app or not?

_____

2 What does Carrie say that shows how she feels about the app?

_____

3 Does Paul like the app or not?

_____

4 What does Paul say that shows how he feels about the app?

_____

B 🔊 **1.01** **LISTEN FOR MAIN POINTS** Listen again. Complete the chart with positives and negatives of facial recognition technology.

Positives	Negatives

2 CRITICAL THINKING

A **THINK CRITICALLY** Who do you think would want to use facial recognition technology? Who do you think would not want to use it? Explain your ideas.

_____

_____

_____

_____

A Complete the conversations with the phrases in the box. Two of the phrases won't be used.

can see how	good point there	guess so	look at it that way
really thought of it	valid point	~~you're coming from~~	you're saying

1 A Robots have advanced so much in the past few years. I think they'll drastically change the way we live in the next five years or so.

   B I get where ____*you're coming from*____ , but I don't think things will change that radically.

2 A I don't like to use virtual assistants. I've heard that everything they hear is recorded and stored. I don't want all of my personal conversations recorded.

   B I hadn't _____ like that. Now I don't know if I want to keep mine.

3 A I hope chatbots don't replace all customer service personnel. I like talking to real people.

   B I understand what _____ , but I think chatbots will help companies save money, and then their goods and services will be cheaper to buy.

4 A I don't think we should let robots do so many different jobs. They'll take jobs away from people.

   B You could _____ , but if robots do simple jobs, humans will be able to do more interesting work.

5 A Language is really complex. Computer translation apps make so many mistakes. That's why I don't like to use them.

   B That's a _____ , but they can be helpful sometimes.

6 A I think I would feel uncomfortable having a robot that looks like a human cooking, cleaning, and walking around in my home. It would be weird.

   B I _____ , but it would be really convenient not to have to cook and clean anymore.

B Write a conversation for each situation. Use the language you practiced in exercise 3A.

1 Anna doesn't like using speech-to-text because there are always so many mistakes. Timo thinks it saves time and helps people who have trouble with their hands.

   Anna _____

   Timo _____

   Anna _____

   Timo _____

2 Michael thinks that everyone should study technology instead of art or literature because technology will be more important in the future. Mila thinks that studying art and literature make us think creatively, and that will help us develop better technology.

   Michael _____

   Mila _____

   Michael _____

   Mila _____

1.4 ROBOTICS TO THE RESCUE

1 READING

A   **PREDICT CONTENT FROM PICTURES** Look at the pictures. What ideas do you think might be explored in this essay? Check (✓) the ideas. Then read the essay and check your answers.

- **a**   benefits of computer translation ☐
- **b**   advantages of speaking multiple languages ☐
- **c**   what human translators do better than computers ☐
- **d**   disadvantages of computer translation ☐
- **e**   costs of human translators vs. computers ☐

ROBOT TRANSLATORS – THEY'RE FASTER, BUT ARE THEY BETTER?

Robots have already become a necessity in some industries. For instance, automobile factories rely on car-building robots for their precision and speed. The mining industry uses robots to mine efficiently and safely. Robotics technology will undoubtedly continue to advance, and robots will be replacing humans in a variety of fields. However, in the field of translation, artificial intelligence is no match for humans.

Computerized translation has its benefits. In situations such as, government meetings and international conferences, computers can translate for hours on end without tiring, unlike human translators. While a person can type an average of about 40 words per minute, a computer can work more than ten times as fast. In addition, a single computer can translate an unlimited number of languages. A person can only translate one language at a time.

Despite the benefits of computer technology, humans will likely always produce better and more accurate translations. First of all, no computer can understand all the slang, idioms, expressions, and local variations in even a single language. For example, how would a robot translate the expression "I've got your back," which does not translate literally? Second, computers can't pick up on things like the subtle differences in the meanings of words, tone, emotion, humor, or sarcasm. For instance, would a robot understand the slang usage of the phrase "give me a ring," which can mean "call me"? Third, language constantly changes. New words are born and existing words take on new meanings. All of these factors can lead to mistranslations and confusion. For these reasons, it will probably be a long time before computers can feasibly replace humans in the field of translation.

B   **READ FOR DETAIL**   Read the essay again. Answer the questions.

1   What reasons does the writer give for stating that computer translation technology is not as good as human translators?

2   According to the writer, what are some benefits of computerized translation?

2 CRITICAL THINKING

A   **THINK CRITICALLY**   Answer the question.

Do you think someone who speaks multiple languages would agree or disagree with this essay? Explain.

3 WRITING

A Circle the correct expressions.

1 In the field of medicine, robots perform a variety of tasks, *just to name a few /* such as dispensing medicine and assisting in surgeries.

2 We're already using robots in our daily lives. *To name a few, / Take, for example,* chatbots.

3 Robots can do things humans can't—lift heavy objects, make extremely fast calculations, and work for 24 hours straight, *just to name a few / namely.*

4 I would love to have a robot in my house to do a lot of things I don't want to do, *like / take, for example,* wash the dishes and clean the bathroom.

5 Many households already use robot technology for housekeeping purposes. *Namely / For instance,* robotic vacuum cleaners are very popular.

B **You are going to write an essay in response to the statement below. Do you agree or disagree with the statement? Organize your ideas in an outline for a three-paragraph essay. Then write your essay.**

Future advances in technology are going to give us more free time.

Paragraph 1: Discussing the statement and its potential consequences

Paragraph 2: Exploring counterarguments

Paragraph 3: Giving a personal opinion

CHECK AND REVIEW

Read the statements. Can you do these things?

UNIT 1	Mark the boxes. ✔ I can do it. ? I am not sure.	If you are not sure, go back to these pages in the Student's Book.
	I can ...	
VOCABULARY	☐ use adverbs to add detail.	page 2
	☐ use words about developments in technology.	page 4
GRAMMAR	☐ use commenting adverbs with future forms.	page 3
	☐ use future perfect and future continuous.	page 5
LISTENING AND SPEAKING SKILLS	☐ listen for attitude in a conversation.	page 6
	☐ acknowledge arguments and propose counterarguments.	page 7
READING AND WRITING SKILLS	☐ read for detail in an article.	page 8
	☐ write an essay about future advances in technology.	page 9

1 VOCABULARY: Describing personality

A **Complete the sentences. Match 1–6 with a–f.**

1 Someone who likes to talk a lot is …   *d*   a   aloof.
2 Someone who is trustworthy and genuine is …   b   narrow-minded.
3 Someone who doesn't accept new or different ideas is …   c   self-centered.
4 Someone who doesn't seem affected by anything is …   d   chatty.
5 Someone who likes to learn about new ideas and try new things is …   e   sincere.
6 Someone who talks only about themselves in conversations is …   f   open-minded.

B **Cross out the word that doesn't belong.**

1   chatty   ~~quiet~~   talkative
2   fake   sincere   genuine
3   unfriendly   open-minded   aloof
4   self-centered   selfish   generous
5   rigid   narrow-minded   accepting
6   insensitive   friendly   selfish
7   aloof   antisocial   chatty

C **Complete the sentences with words from the box.**

| ~~aloof~~   chatty   narrow-minded   open-minded   self-centered   sincere |

1 People often think I'm _____*aloof*_____ because I don't talk very much.
2 It's difficult to talk about new ideas with _____ people.
   They have a hard time understanding things that they aren't familiar with.
3 John is so _____. He only thinks about himself.
4 If Alice tells you that she likes something, you can believe her.
   She's always very _____.
5 I'm trying to be more _____
   and accept people the way they are.
6 I like Andrew, but he is so

   _____.
   Sometimes I just need quiet time.

2 GRAMMAR: Uses of *will*

A **Read the assumptions or deductions below. Are they about the past or the present?**

1 If it's noon, Marco will not have have eaten lunch yet.   ___past___

2 Tomas will do every personality quiz he finds online.   _____

3 James will usually be on social media in the mornings.   _____

4 Karen will have posted all of these photos on social media by the end of the day.   _____

5 If Kim is at home, she won't be studying.   _____

6 Ling will be at work or at school in the afternoons.   _____

B **Read the sentences about people at a party. (Circle) the correct words to complete the sentences.**

1 Don't worry about leaving Kelly alone at a party. She's chatty and outgoing. *(She'll have)/ She'll* met everyone in the room in the first ten minutes.

2 People *will / will be* think Luis is aloof, but he's just quiet.

3 Lauren *won't / won't be* make small talk. She likes to make sincere connections with people, so *she'll / she'll be* having very intense conversations.

4 Carl can be a little self-centered, so *he'll / he'll be* talking about himself at any party he goes to.

5 Jonas is not very open-minded, so *he won't / he won't have* continue to talk to people who disagree with him.

6 Ian is narrow-minded, so *he'll be / he'll have* decided who he's going to talk to before the party even starts.

3 GRAMMAR AND VOCABULARY

A **Write sentences about how different people will behave at a party this Saturday. Use the cues in parentheses.**

1 A narrow-minded person (*will* + verb) will stay away from people that look different.

2 An open-minded person (*will* + verb) _____

3 A chatty person (*will* + *have* + past participle) _____

4 A self-centered person (*will* + *be* + *ing*) _____

5 A sincere person (*will* + *have* + past participle) _____

6 An aloof person (*will* + *be* + *ing*) _____

1 VOCABULARY: Using three-word phrasal verbs

A Complete each three-word phrasal verb with a missing word from the box. One of the words is used twice.

against	around	back	down	for	in	~~through~~	to	up

1 It's difficult to **get** _____through_____ **to** her sometimes.
2 Why do you **put** _____ **with** bad employees?
3 He tends to **look** _____ **on** others because he thinks he's better than everyone.
4 Why do I always **run up** _____ the same problems?
5 You have to **stand up** _____ what you believe in.
6 Don't take him seriously. He likes to **mess** _____ **with** people.
7 It will all **come** _____ **to** our company's main goal.
8 The new employees **fit** _____ **with** our team members really well.
9 Do you have a job to **fall** _____ **on** if this new idea doesn't work out?
10 You have to **face up** _____ your problems.

B Write the correct three-word phrasal verb from exercise 1A next to each definition.

1 feel that you belong _____fit in with_____
2 tolerate _____
3 think you are better than someone _____
4 experience difficulties _____
5 communicate successfully _____
6 joke with _____
7 be the most important part _____
8 defend _____
9 deal with _____
10 do something easy or familiar _____

2 GRAMMAR: Uses of *would*

A Match 1–6 with a–f.

1 He asked me if I would let him borrow twenty dollars. ___
2 I would take that job. ___
3 When we were young, we'd play in the park together. ___
4 Would you mind opening the door for me? ___
5 I think he's a great guy, but he wouldn't be right for that job. ___
6 It's not surprising that he would want to leave early. He doesn't like parties. ___

a refer to a past habit
b make a polite request
c express an opinion in a polite way
d report a statement or question
e talk about something that is expected or typical
f talk about what someone is willing or unwilling to do

B   **Read the sentences. Then (circle) the best next sentence.**

1   Lucas is always so rude to you.

    a I wouldn't put up with it if I were you.   **b** He asked me if I would talk to you.

2   I can't get through to Mike.

    a Would you mind talking to him for me?   **b** I wouldn't do that if I were you.

3   Julia can't face up to her money problems.

    a It's natural that she would want to avoid talking about them.   **b** She asked me if I would talk about them.

4   He made a lot of money as a computer programmer.

    a He'd always talk about changing jobs.   **b** It's understandable that he would fall back on that job.

5   You're always messing around with Pedro, and it hurts his feelings.

    a You'd think he would be nicer to you.   **b** Would you try to be nicer to him?

3   GRAMMAR AND VOCABULARY

A   **Rewrite each underlined sentence. Use *would* and the cue in parentheses. Make any other necessary changes to the sentence.**

1   When I was young, I didn't fit in with other kids. <u>I liked to play by myself.</u>

    (talk about a past habit) I would play by myself.

2   He likes to mess around with people all the time. <u>I don't think he's a good candidate for a teaching job.</u>

    (express an opinion in a polite way) _____

3   I lost Kim's house keys, and I can't face up to her. <u>Do you think you could tell her for me?</u>

    (make a polite request) _____

4   She has to work late tonight. <u>She wants me to look in on her mother for her.</u>

    (report a statement or question) _____

5   You're good at standing up to bullies. <u>I'm not surprised that he called you about his problem with the kids at school.</u>

    (talk about something expected or typical) _____

6   Their neighbors are so loud. <u>I don't think I could put up with it.</u>

    (talk about what someone is willing or unwilling to do) _____

2.3 SAME HERE!

1 LISTENING

A 🔊 **2.01** **Listen and circle the correct answers.**

1 Sam wants Cathy to _____ .
   a go to the beach with him
   b get a job at his office
   c join a soccer team

2 When Cathy was young, people _____ .
   a thought she was good at sports
   b didn't think she was good at sports
   c didn't think she was good at school

3 When Sam was young, people _____ .
   a thought he disliked sports
   b didn't think he was good at sports
   c didn't think he was good at school

4 Sam and Cathy _____ .
   a had the exact same experience when they were young
   b had different experiences that made them feel the same
   c had different experiences and don't understand each other

B 🔊 **2.01** **LISTEN FOR AGREEMENT** **Listen again. Then read the sentences and write *T* (true) or *F* (false).**

1 Sam wants Cathy to join a team at work. ⎽T⎽
2 Sam has never seen Cathy play soccer. ____
3 Cathy looks like a typical athlete. ____
4 Sam looks like a typical athlete. ____
5 Teachers accused Sam of cheating in school. ____
6 Sam went to the beach last weekend. ____
7 Sam and Cathy are going to go to the beach together this weekend. ____

2 CRITICAL THINKING

A **THINK CRITICALLY** **Do you think people judge others based on the way they look? Have you ever judged people based on how they look? Explain.**

_____

_____

_____

_____

_____

SPEAKING

A   **Complete the conversation with the missing words.**

coincidence	experience	hear	here	just	mean	relate

Max	Are you going to Hassan's annual picnic on Saturday, Jan?
Jan	No, I don't think so. Are you?
Max	No, I don't like big group events. They make me so tired.
Jan	Same ¹_____! If I went to the picnic, I'd have to rest all day Sunday.
Max	I know exactly what you ²_____. I went to the picnic last year. It was a lot of fun, but I had to stay home and watch movies by myself the whole next day.
Jan	That's ³_____ like the time I went to my college reunion. I spent the next day watching movies and reading. I just like spending time alone, I guess.
Max	I ⁴_____ you. I love spending time alone. I did a personality quiz once, and I found out I'm an introvert.
Jan	What a ⁵_____! I'm an introvert, too. And introverts aren't shy or aloof like people think.
Max	That's right. We just need more alone time than other people do.
Jan	Yeah, I need a lot of alone time. My husband, Peter, doesn't though. He's an extrovert. He loves being around other people.
Max	I can ⁶_____ to that. My best friend Rick always wants to go to parties. He finally stopped asking me to go with him. Has that been your ⁷_____ with your husband?
Jan	Yes, exactly. He used to try to get me to go to parties with him all the time, but he finally gave up.

B   **Imagine that Max's best friend, Rick, and Jan's husband, Peter, are talking. They want to go to Hassan's picnic. Write their conversation. Use at least two phrases to discuss similar experiences.**

Rick   Max doesn't want to go to Hassan's picnic on Saturday, but I do. It was really fun last year.

Peter   _____

_____

Rick   _____

_____

Peter   _____

_____

2.4 READ THE LABEL

1 READING

A **PREDICT CONTEXT** Look at the picture. What is the person doing? Read the headline of the article. What do you think the article will be about?

1 The person is

_____ .

2 I think the article will be about

_____ .

A LOT OF WORK FOR NOTHING?

A lot of work goes into creating a nutrition label. Calorie, fat, sugar, and nutrient content must be carefully measured for accuracy so that consumers can make informed decisions about what they eat and feed their families. However, consumers can only benefit from that information if they actually read the labels. Recently, two groups of researchers were curious about whether or not people do read nutrition labels.

One of the studies, which was conducted by the United States Food and Drug Administration, found that 50% of US adults say that they read nutrition labels all or most of the time. That means that 50% report not reading them most of the time. The study reveals that twelve percent of adults say they rarely read the labels, and surprisingly, 10% claim never to read them.

A study led by researchers at the University of Minnesota focused on which label components participants looked at. Thirty-three percent of participants said that they usually read the calorie content. Between 24% and 31% said that they read the fat, sugar, and serving size information on nutrition labels. But were the participants reporting their behavior accurately? The researchers used eye trackers to see which parts of the labels participants were actually reading. The eye-tracker data indicated that only 9% of participants read the calorie count, and a mere 1% looked at calorie, fat, sugar, and serving size information.

Why don't people actually read nutrition labels? One reason may be that they are printed in small type that may be hard to read. Another reason may be that there is too much information on them to understand them easily. Whatever the reason, the data would suggest that nutrition labels are not as effective and useful as we might have hoped they would be.

B **IDENTIFY PURPOSE** Answer the questions.

1 What do you think is the writer's main intention in this article?

  a to entertain   **b** to inform   **c** to share personal information

2 Who do you think is the target audience for the article?

  a the general public   **b** researchers   **c** the Food and Drug Administration

2 CRITICAL THINKING

A **THINK CRITICALLY** Why do you think people's reported behavior did not match their actual behavior?

_____

_____

_____

3 WRITING

A Look at the bar graph. Complete each sentence. Use the words in the box and the correct percentage.

| indices | observed | ~~reveals that~~ | shows that |

1 The graph ___reveals that 18%___
   don't think food labels are important.

2 As can be _____
   buy what their family likes.

3 The graph _____
   are happy with their health and diet.

4 The data _____
   get product information from other sources.

B Write a paragraph about the graph in exercise A.
Use expressions for referring to data.

Why do some people never read labels?

WHY PEOPLE DON'T READ NUTRITION LABELS
(Participants were allowed to choose more than one answer.)

LABELS NOT IMPORTANT

BUY WHAT FAMILY LIKES

HAPPY WITH HEALTH AND DIET

GET NUTRITION INFORMATION SOMEWHERE ELSE

0   10   20   30   40   50   60   70   80

CHECK AND REVIEW

Read the statements. Can you do these things?

UNIT 2

Mark the boxes. ☑ I can do it. ? I am not sure.		If you are not sure, go back to these pages in the Student's Book.
	I can ...	
VOCABULARY	☐ use personality adjectives.	page 12
	☐ use three-word phrasal verbs.	page 14
GRAMMAR	☐ use *will* in different situations.	page 13
	☐ use *would* in different situations.	page 15
LISTENING AND SPEAKING SKILLS	☐ listen for detail in a conversation.	page 17
	☐ use expressions to discuss and compare similar experiences.	page 17
READING AND WRITING SKILLS	☐ read a report based on data.	page 18
	☐ write a paragraph about a graph.	page 19

3.1   I TOLD YOU SO!

A (Circle) the answer that completes each sentence. There may be more than one acceptable answer.

1 Let's _____ all of our options before we make our decision.

    a reject   **(b)** reconsider   **(c)** review

2 I didn't like his idea at all, so I _____ it and tried to think of a better idea.

    a rejected   **b** dismissed   **c** disregarded

3 Do you _____ any problems with our plan?

    a presume   **b** foresee   **c** envision

4 We can't _____ that everything will work out the way we hope. There might be problems that we didn't think about.

    a presume   **b** interpret   **c** dismiss

5 I'm not sure why our plan didn't work. I think we should _____ the situation and figure out what we did wrong.

    a presume   **b** analyze   **c** evaluate

6 How do you _____ the situation? Where do you think we made mistakes?

    a foresee   **b** envision   **c** interpret

7 It's good to look at a situation and try to figure out where it went wrong, but you shouldn't _____ on it.

    a interpret   **b** fixate   **c** reconsider

B **Complete each sentence with words from the box.**

analyze	dismiss	disregard	envision	evaluate	foresee

1 If you want to understand a future situation, you try to _____ , or _____ , what will happen.

2 If you think someone is wrong about a future situation, you might _____ , or _____ , what they say.

3 If you want to look carefully at what happened in a past situation, you would _____ , or _____ , the event.

2 GRAMMAR: Variations on past unreal conditionals

A **Match the sentence halves.**

1 You'd have finished it by now … ___d___   a if I'd known you were in town.
2 If you'd asked me earlier, … _____   b I'd have been able to go with you.
3 We'd have arrived on time … _____   c I would've said something.
4 I'd have invited you … _____   d if you'd been working on it all week.
5 If you hadn't driven so fast, … _____   e if you hadn't taken that phone call.
6 If I'd been there, … _____   f you wouldn't have been in an accident.

B **Complete the sentences with the correct forms of the verbs in parentheses.**

1 If he _____had said_____ (say) that to me, I _____would've been_____ (be) really angry.
2 I _____ (got) you a sandwich, if I _____ (know) you were home.
3 If I _____ (not / see) it with my own eyes, I _____ (think) he had made it all up.
4 You _____ (not / got) sick if you _____ (not / sit) next to the woman who was coughing and sneezing.
5 If you _____ (come) to the lake with us, you _____ (have) a great time.
6 We _____ (walk) here if it _____ (not / rain) so hard.

3 GRAMMAR AND VOCABULARY

A **Write sentences about the situations below. Use the verb in parentheses, a past unreal conditional, and your own ideas.**

1 The project didn't go as planned. (analyze)
   If I had analyzed the schedule, the project would have gone better _____ .
2 I didn't listen to my friend's advice. (disregard)
   If I hadn't _____ .
3 Henry didn't think about what went wrong with his last job. (evaluate)
   If Henry had _____ .
4 You thought about potential problems. (foresee)
   You'd have _____ .
5 Sonia believed the weather warnings and packed an umbrella. (dismiss)
   If she'd _____ .

GO WITH THE FLOW

1 VOCABULARY: Describing emotional reactions

A **Cross out the word that doesn't belong.**

1	composed	flustered	mellow	**4**	successful	victorious	defeated
2	melodramatic	hysterical	victorious	**5**	helpless	resourceful	inventive
3	defensive	harmless	innocent	**6**	spiteful	gracious	forgiving

B **Write the correct words from exercise 1A next to the definitions. You won't use all of the words.**

1 not hurting anyone _____

2 kind and understanding when other people make mistakes _____ , _____

3 showing extreme emotion _____ , _____

4 able to solve problems creatively _____

5 not getting excited or upset in a difficult situation _____ , _____

6 wanting to upset or hurt someone _____

7 nervous or upset _____

C **Complete the sentences with words from exercise 1B.**

1 I was so _____ after the car accident that I couldn't remember my telephone number!

2 John is always so _____ . He never gets upset, even when something goes really wrong.

3 Don't be so _____ . I'm sure you're not going to lose your job just because you spilled coffee on your boss.

4 Wow, I can't believe you were able to find a new location for the company retreat in just two days. You're so _____ !

5 I heard that you got the promotion that Mark wanted. Be careful. He can be _____ when he feels that he's been treated unfairly.

2 GRAMMAR: Commenting on the past

A **Find the errors and rewrite the sentences.**

1 You should have saw the movie with us.

_____

_____

2 They may not heard you.

_____

3 I might been studying all night.

_____

4 He could have get angry.

_____

5 It shouldn't have been ate.

_____

B **Circle the correct answers to complete the sentences.**

1 The soccer game was great. You *should have been / might have been* there.

2 William didn't come to Andy's birthday party. He *should not have gotten / may not have gotten* the invitation.

3 Wow, this TV is a lot cheaper here than it was online. We *couldn't have bought / shouldn't have bought* it at that store.

4 I tried to call Annie a few times last weekend to see if she wanted to hang out, but she didn't answer her phone. She *may have been working / should have been working* all weekend.

5 I heard you almost got a job at my company last year. We *should have been working / could have been working* together all this time!

3 GRAMMAR AND VOCABULARY

A **Complete the conversation. Use expressions of exaggeration or understatement and *have* + your own ideas.**

Kim I was driving to a job interview this morning, and right before I got there, the guy in front of me was driving so slowly in the parking lot.

Marco He could ¹_____.

Kim Yeah, he was looking for a parking spot, but I yelled at him. I was almost late and I was already stressed about the interview, so I got a little ²_____ and told him that it would be his fault if I didn't get the job. Then, when I got to the interview, the interviewer was the guy in the car!

Marco Oh, no! He might not ³_____.

Kim He did recognize me. He was very ⁴_____ and laughed about it, but I was so embarrassed.

Marco How did the interview go?

Kim It was horrible. I was really ⁵_____ so I kept dropping things and forgetting what I wanted to say. I know I didn't get the job.

Marco You shouldn't ⁶_____.

Kim I know. I should have been more patient. Believe me, I'm never going to yell at another driver again.

A COMPLETE DISASTER!

1 LISTENING

A 🔊 **3.01** **LISTEN FOR ATTITUDE** **Listen to the conversation between Serena and her friend Zach. Then answer the questions.**

1 Who did Serena have a meeting with?

_____

2 How did her meeting go?

_____

3 How does Serena feel about the situation?

_____

4 How does Zach react to the story?

_____

B 🔊 **3.01** **LISTEN FOR DETAILS** **Listen to the conversation again. Check (✓) the things that happened. Write (✗) next to the things that didn't happen.**

Serena showed her boss summaries of her projects for the year. ☐

Serena said something bad about a co-worker. ☐

Serena was late for her meeting with her boss. ☐

Serena asked for a raise and a promotion. ☐

Serena was in another meeting. ☐

The boss said Serena could have the raise, but not the promotion. ☐

Serena realized that she forgot to bring something to the meeting. ☐

Serena asked her boss for a new project idea. ☐

2 CRITICAL THINKING

A 🔊 **3.02** **THINK CRITICALLY** **Listen to a conversation between Serena and her mother. Then answer the questions.**

1 What are three ways Serena's conversation with her mother is different from her conversation with Zach?

_____

_____

_____

2 What are two possible reasons that Serena's conversation with her mother is different from her conversation with Zach?

_____

_____

3 SPEAKING

A   **Look at the clues and complete the crossword.**

ACROSS

4   It was the worst presentation ___!

5   It was a(n) ___ disaster.

7   Everything that could ___ go wrong did go wrong.

8   I just couldn't ___ this was happening!

DOWN

1   I think you're blowing it out of ___ .

2   You haven't heard the ___ part yet.

3   We've all been ___ .

6   I'll bet no one even ___ .

B   **Write a short conversation for each situation below. Use some of the phrases from exercise 3A.**

1   You tried out for the baseball team this morning. You haven't played in a while, so you couldn't hit the ball and you missed almost every catch. You tell your friend about it.

    You _____

    Your friend _____

    You _____

    Your friend _____

2   Your neighbor is upset because he cooked dinner for his boss last night and it was bad. He burned the chicken, the soup was too salty, and he spilled soda on his boss's expensive jacket.

    Your neighbor _____

    You _____

    Your neighbor _____

    You _____

    Your neighbor _____

3.4 TOO STRANGE TO BE TRUE?

1 READING

A **CREATE COHESION** Read the headline of the first story. What do you think it's about? Complete the statement. Then read the story to check your answer.

I think it's about _____ .

ABRAHAM LINCOLN AND JOHN F. KENNEDY: Parallel Lives?

Abraham Lincoln and John F. Kennedy were both American presidents. But the similarities between them don't stop there. Read on and find out about the remarkable coincidences in the lives and deaths of the two men.

- Lincoln became president in 1860. Kennedy had that same honor in 1960.
- The names Lincoln and Kennedy both contain seven letters.
- Both presidents were assassinated on a Friday.
- Lincoln's secretary, Kennedy, warned him not to go to the theater, where he was assassinated. Kennedy's secretary, Lincoln, warned him not to go to Dallas, where he would later be killed.
- Both their assassins were known by three names: John Wilkes Booth and Lee Harvey Oswald.
- Both men were succeeded as president by men named Johnson—Andrew and Lyndon B.

THE LINCOLN AND KENNEDY COINCIDENCES: Are they as amazing as they seem?

The long list of coincidences between Abraham Lincoln and John F. Kennedy has been circulating on the Internet for several years now. How accurate is this list? Let's examine the facts:

- The two men were elected president 100 years apart, which is no more than a satisfying round number. US Presidential elections occur every four years, or 25 times per century.
- The average length of US Presidents' names is 6.6 letters, so 7 letters is not uncommon. Also, their first names do not contain the same number of letters.
- Because there are only seven days in a week, there is a one in seven chance that they would have been assassinated on the same day of the week. In addition, the actual dates of their assassinations are different. Lincoln died on April 15, 1865 while Kennedy died on November 22, 1963.
- There is no record of Abraham Lincoln having had a secretary named Kennedy. John F. Kennedy did, indeed, have a secretary named Evelyn Lincoln, but there is no proof that she warned him not to go to Dallas. In addition, both men may have been warned on the days they were killed, but both had been warned several other times not to attend events because of threats to their lives.
- Before Kennedy's assassination, Lee Harvey Oswald went by the name Lee, not Lee Harvey. His middle name was used publicly only after the assassination. In addition, many Americans have three names—a first, a middle, and a last name.
- It's true that after both men's deaths, men named Johnson became president. However, Johnson is one of the most popular surnames in the United States. It is currently the second most common surname in the country.

B **EVALUATE CONTENT** Read the story and the report from a fact-checking site. Then complete the chart.

Which coincidences in the story are true?	Which are untrue?

2 CRITICAL THINKING

A **THINK CRITICALLY** Which facts make the coincidences in the story seem less significant? List two of these facts below and explain how each one lessens the impact of the story's coincidences.

1 Fact: _____

Explanation: _____

2 Fact: _____

Explanation: _____

3 WRITING

A Complete the sentences with words from the box. Not all words are used.

both	each	neither	same	together	two

1 Their last names have the _____ number of letters. _____ has seven letters.

2 _____ men were assassinated on a Friday.

3 _____ man ever served as vice-president.

4 The _____ presidents were succeeded by men named Johnson.

B Write a new version of the story about Lincoln and Kennedy's coincidences. Include only facts and use the words in exercise 3A to point out coincidences.

_____

_____

_____

_____

CHECK AND REVIEW

Read the statements. Can you do these things?

UNIT 3	Mark the boxes. ✔ I can do it. ? I am not sure. I can ...	If you are not sure, go back to these pages in the Student's Book.
VOCABULARY	☐ use words that describe thought processes. ☐ describe emotional reactions.	page 22 page 24
GRAMMAR	☐ use past unreal conditionals. ☐ comment on the past.	page 23 page 25
LISTENING AND SPEAKING SKILLS	☐ listen for attitude in a conversation. ☐ offer sympathy and reassurance.	page 26 page 27
READING AND WRITING SKILLS	☐ read two stories and evaluate their content. ☐ write a short paragraph based on facts.	page 29 page 29

1 VOCABULARY: Describing things

A Write a word from the box that has the same or the opposite meaning. You will not use one of the words.

circular	cylindrical	delicate	elaborate	filthy	flaky
miniature	multicolored	ridged	~~spiral~~	stringy	

The same meaning

1 twisting _____spiral_____

2 round _____

3 tube-shaped _____

4 crumbly _____

5 colorful _____

The opposite meaning

6 mammoth _____

7 clean _____

8 strong _____

9 smooth _____

10 simple _____

B Complete the sentences with words from exercise 1A.

1 Microphotography can make tiny things look _____ .

2 The _____ wings of a butterfly, which normally don't look very strong, can look like iron gates in a microphotograph.

3 A microphotograph might reveal that something that normally looks tan or brown, such as sand, is actually _____ .

4 Something that looks basic, like a fly's eye, might really be very _____ and complex.

5 Something that appears to be dirt-free might, in fact, look _____ close up.

2 GRAMMAR: Quantifiers and prepositions in relative clauses

A (Circle) the correct phrase to complete the sentences.

1 Insect bodies, *most of which / each of which / many of whom* look smooth to the naked eye, can look rough up close.

2 Microphotography can surprise people, *most of which / many of whom / each of whom* have never wondered what insects look like up close.

3 Insects, *each of which / most of whom / many of which* have intricately formed wings and eyes, are more complex than they seem.

4 Microphotographs of bees, for instance, allow us to see their eyes, *most of which / many of which / each of which* is covered in tiny hairs.

5 Microphotographs of insects were shown to some people, *each of which / most of whom / most of which* could not guess what the photos depicted.

B **Correct the mistakes in the sentences.**

1   My friends, most of ~~which~~ *whom* go to my school, are coming to my birthday party.

2   I don't know what happened in the movie, which I wasn't really paying attention.

3   We enjoyed all of the dishes, each of them had been prepared by a different person.

4   I finally finished the homework, which I just found out about it.

5   My closet is full of clothes, which most of them I never wear.

C **Read the art review. Complete the online article with *each/many/most/all/none/*or *some + of* and *which* or *whom*.**
Different answers may be possible.

> Tonight, I'm at a photography exhibition titled "Up Close and Personal." It's an exhibition of microphotography.
> A lot of the exhibitors come from the world of science. Microphotographers, [1] _____
> are scientists, but [2] _____ are not, are interested in seeing what things look like close up.
>
> The microphotos, [3] _____ show us an object or a living thing from a different
> perspective, are fascinating to look at. A photo of sand, for example, shows us individual grains,
> [4] _____ has its own unique shape.
>
> Exhibition-goers can't buy the photos, [5] _____ are for sale. After the exhibition in the
> gallery, the photos are going to be donated to museums, [6] _____ are science-based.
> These museums want to get their visitors interested in science.

3 GRAMMAR AND VOCABULARY

A **Read some more sentences from the art review and complete the sentences with your own ideas.**
Use the phrases in parentheses.

1   (are elaborate and) The photos, each of which offers us a close-up view of a different subject,
    are elaborate and show us the world from a different perspective .

2   (all of which) From the position of a photography fan, I couldn't choose a favorite from among the photos,

    .

3   (all of whom) We had a chance to learn about the photos from the standpoint of the photographers,

    .

4   (mammoth) The photos of plants and flowers, all of which were beautiful,

    .

5   (miniature) Microphotographers, many of whom are scientists,

    .

EYE TO EYE

1 VOCABULARY: Eye idioms and metaphors

A **Match each idiom or metaphor with its meaning.**

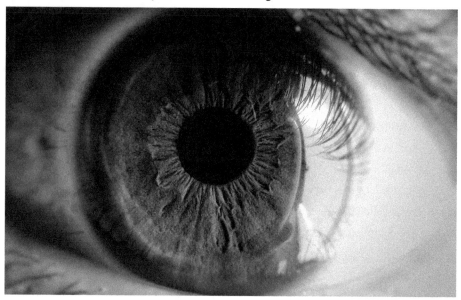

1	a bird's eye view of something	___	a	to remember to think about the end goal
2	feast your eyes on something	___	b	to attract someone
3	see eye to eye on something	___	c	a view from above
4	keep your eyes on the prize	___	d	to ignore an illegal or harmful activity
5	turn a blind eye to something	___	e	to look at something with great pleasure
6	catch somebody's eye	___	f	to agree with someone
7	in the public eye	___	g	famous and in view of the whole world
8	in your mind's eye	___	h	without hesitation
9	without batting an eye	___	i	to be aware of everything that is happening
10	have eyes in the back of your head	___	j	in your imagination
11	in the blink of an eye	___	k	instantly

B **Complete each sentence with the correct form of an idiom or metaphor from exercise 1A.**

1 I think my mother _has eyes in the back of her head_ . I can never hide anything from her.

2 She must have a lot of money. She paid $5,000 for that ring _____ .

3 Jackie and I don't _____ . We disagree all the time.

4 That photo really _____ . I think it's beautiful.

5 He was gone _____ . I turned away for one second, and when I turned back around he had disappeared.

6 I would hate to live my life _____ . I don't know how celebrities deal with it.

7 I can't remember the address of the gallery, but I can see it _____ . It's a black building with a red door.

8 It seems the police have decided to _____ the fact that people always speed on this road. I guess they don't think it's a big deal.

2 GRAMMAR: Noun clauses with question words

A   For each noun or noun phrase, write a question word that you can use as a substitute.

1 the people _____   3 reasons _____   5 the place _____

2 things _____   4 the way _____

B   Rewrite each sentence with the question word in parentheses.

1 I'm amazed by all of the things that the human eye can do.

(what) I'm amazed by what the human eye can do _____ .

2 It's interesting to see the ways that different animals' eyes developed.

(how) _____ .

3 There are so many interesting facts to share about eyes that I'm not sure which fact to begin with.

(what) _____ .

4 Because eyes are so unique, we can use them to prove that we are the people that we say we are.

(who) _____ .

5 No one really knows the reasons that the human eye developed the way it did.

(why) _____ .

6 The photographers explained the way they took their photos.

(how) _____ .

3 GRAMMAR AND VOCABULARY

A   Complete the sentences to write an advertisement for a museum exhibit about eyes.

Come to **THE MICROPHOTOGRAPHY EXHIBIT** *at the Science Museum!*

Feast your eyes on [1] _____ .
Find out why [2] _____ .
Learn how [3] _____ .
See what [4] _____ .
Get a bird's eye view of [5] _____ .

Beautiful photos of eyes!

Why can't we see colors in the dark?

How do eagles and tigers see?

What do sharks and eagles see?

What does the world look like from an eagle's perspective?

LOOK AWAY!

1 LISTENING

A ◀)) **4.01** **LISTEN FOR MAIN IDEA** **Listen to the first half of the podcast. Then write answers to the questions.**

1 What does Samantha want to know?

2 What harmful activity does Dr. Chang talk about?

B ◀)) **4.01** **LISTEN FOR DETAILS** **Listen again and read the statements. Write *T* for true or *F* for false.**

1 You'll damage your eyes anytime you go outside without eye protection. ___

2 Going out regularly without sun protection can lead to eye diseases, cancer, and vision damage. ___

3 Summer is the most important time of year to wear sunglasses. ___

4 In the winter, the risk of sun damage to your eyes is higher if there's snow outside. ___

5 You need sunglasses with UV protection to protect your eyes. ___

C ◀)) **4.02** **LISTEN FOR DETAILS** **Listen to the second half of the podcast. Then check (✓) all the correct answers.**

According to Dr. Chang, rubbing your eyes is a bad habit because

☐ you can scratch your eyes.

☐ you can get allergies.

☐ you have germs on your hands.

☐ you can get an eye infection.

☐ you can damage your corneas.

☐ you can develop certain eye conditions, such as myopia or glaucoma.

☐ you can break blood vessels around your eyes.

2 SPEAKING

A   Complete the sentences with expressions from the box. Not all expressions will be used.

> comes down to
> getting at the heart of
> in itself
> key to
> major impact
> objectively
> straightforward
> there's considerably more to it
> truth of the matter is

Samantha   Can we talk about diet and how it affects eye health?

Dr. Chang   Ah, now we're ¹ _____ how our daily habits affect our eyes. Your diet can have a ² _____ on your eye health. The ³ _____ having healthy eyes is eating foods rich in certain nutrients, such as Vitamin C, lutein, zinc, and omega-3 fatty acids.

Samantha   I see. Is there anything else we should be aware of?

Dr. Chang   Well, the issue is pretty ⁴ _____ . If you're not getting the vitamins and minerals that you need, it's not likely that your eyes will be healthy.

Samantha   Are there any common household items that can harm our eyes?

Dr. Chang   The ⁵ _____ there are a lot of chemicals in the average home that can cause severe eye damage. Household cleaners, for instance, can cause a variety of problems from mild irritation to loss of vision.

Samantha   How can we avoid injuring our eyes when we're cleaning?

Dr. Chang   It really ⁶ _____ protecting your eyes any time you work with dangerous chemicals.

B   Think of three things you've learned in this unit about keeping your eyes healthy. Then write a conversation, giving someone advice about how to keep his/her eyes healthy. Use at least three expressions from exercise 2A.

A   What are some tips for keeping my eyes healthy? _____

B   _____

A   _____

B   _____

A   _____

B   _____

A   _____

B   _____

31

4.4 ATTENTION TO DETAIL

1 READING

A **READ FOR MAIN IDEA** Read the blog post. Which sentence best summarizes the whole post? Underline it.

Seeing Things from a Different Perspective

Do you tend to get stuck in details and forget about the big picture? Being detail-oriented can help you get things done, but if you focus exclusively on details, you might never accomplish, or even think about, your bigger life goals. The good news is that your attention to detail can actually help you reach your life goals once you've defined them.

The first step in improving your ability to see the big picture is to actually devote time to the task. It can be easy to become so focused on details that you go from one small task to another without taking a break. Take some time out of each day to stop and think about your big goals. For example, is there a career that you want to have in the future? Do you want to

get a degree? Do you want to write a book, live in a different city, become fluent in a new language? Envision yourself having achieved that goal.

Now, this is where your attention to detail comes into play. With your eventual outcome clear in your mind's eye, list the steps that you have to take to meet your goal. Writing details on sticky notes, sticking them on a wall, and looking at them all together might help you get a bird's eye view of the situation.

Finally, write your big goal down and post it somewhere where you can see it every day. The daily reminder will help you remember to keep your eyes on the prize and not get so buried in details that you lose sight of your ultimate goal.

B **READ FOR DETAILS** Complete the summary of the blog post with phrases from the box. **Not all phrases will be used.**

see the big picture	thinking about
achieving those goals	talking about
focus on details	time for reaching
steps toward achieving	writing it down

You can use your ability to [1] _____ to achieve big-picture life goals. First, spend time [2] _____ your life goals and see yourself [3] _____. Next, consider the necessary [4] _____ your big goals. Finally, remind yourself of that big-picture goal every day by [5] _____ and putting it somewhere you can see it.

2 CRITICAL THINKING

A **THINK CRITICALLY** Write an answer to the question.

What other kinds of goals do you think the tips in the blog post could help you achieve? Explain.

_____

_____

32

3 WRITING

A **Put the words in the correct order to complete the phrases.**

1 track / record / successful

with a _____

2 problems / practical / to / solving / approach

with a _____

3 marketing / double / major / and business / in

as a _____

4 world / startups / to dot-com

from the corporate

_____

5 for / eye / keen / detail

with a _____

B **Choose one of the jobs from the box and list the skills and qualities that you think it requires. Then write a personal statement for an ideal candidate for the job you chose. Make your statement clear and concise.**

office manager for a busy lawyer's office   volunteer coordinator for a high school
computer programmer for an app developer   visiting nurse (visiting patients at home)

Skills and Qualities:

_____

_____

Ideal Candidate:

_____

_____

CHECK AND REVIEW

Read the statements. Can you do these things?

UNIT 4	Mark the boxes. ☑ I can do it. ? I am not sure. I can ...		If you are not sure, go back to these pages in the Student's Book.
VOCABULARY	☐ describe things.		page 34
	☐ use eye idioms and metaphors.		page 36
GRAMMAR	☐ use quantifiers and prepositions in relative clauses.		page 35
	☐ use noun clauses with question words.		page 37
LISTENING AND SPEAKING SKILLS	☐ listen for details in a podcast.		page 38
	☐ clarify a problem and give advice.		page 39
READING AND WRITING SKILLS	☐ read for gist and detail in a blog post.		page 40
	☐ write a personal statement for a job candidate.		page 41

UNIT 5 REMOTE

5.1 THE END OF THE ROAD

1 VOCABULARY: Describing remote places

A **Cross out the word that is different in meaning.**

1	~~crowded~~	barren	deserted
2	unspoiled	untouched	ruined
3	immense	isolated	vast
4	well-known	anonymous	nameless

5	scenic	ugly	beautiful
6	bare	lush	abundant
7	harsh	friendly	hostile

B **Circle the best word to complete each sentence.**

1 It's easy to get lost in the forest if you don't know where you're going because it's … .

    a immense   **b** nameless   **c** unspoiled

2 A lot of people go to the mountains to enjoy the … landscape.

    a barren   **b** hostile   **c** scenic

3 The desert can be a very … place. It is often extremely hot in the daylight hours and freezing cold at night.

    a picturesque   **b** hostile   **c** abundant

4 It's difficult to find a place that is … . Most places have been visited by people.

    a vast   **b** unspoiled   **c** abandoned

5 The area around the lake was … with trees, plants, and flowers.

    a barren   **b** deserted   **c** lush

2 GRAMMAR: Participle phrases in initial position

A **Check (✓) the correct sentences. Then correct the mistakes in the incorrect sentences.**

1 Having ~~to lose~~ *lost* our map, we couldn't find our way out of the forest. ☐

2 Exhausting from climbing, we finally reached the top of the hill. ☐

3 Sitting at the top of the hill, we could see a vast scenic landscape in front of us. ☐

4 Amazed at the beauty of our surroundings, we were speechless. ☐

5 Having to find a quiet peaceful spot to rest, we put down our packs and had lunch. ☐

6 Looking for unspoiled locations they traveled all over the country. ☐

B **Put the words in the correct order to make sentences. Start each sentence with a participle phrase. Add commas in the correct places.**

1 spot to / a remote / camp / we found / wandering / through the woods

   Wandering through the woods, we found a remote spot to camp.

2 the spot we found / our tents / we started / excited / putting up / by

   _____

3 wood for / having set / began / to gather / up our tents / a fire / we

   _____

4 of / our dinner / the fire / seated / in front / we cooked

   _____

5 scary stories / and told / having / we / relaxed / eaten dinner

   _____

6 we went / of hiking / long day / to sleep / tired / from a / early

   _____

7 our tents / we heard / animals / lying in / of forest / the sounds

   _____

3 GRAMMAR AND VOCABULARY

A **Write sentences about the two photos below using the prompts. Start each sentence with a participle phrase.**

1 walk through the immense area / you

   Walking through the immense area, you might get lost.

2 unspoiled by humans / the forest

   _____

3 find this scenic place / you

   _____

4 deserted decades ago / the town

   _____

5 look at the town now / it's hard to believe / it

   _____

6 abandon their homes / residents

   _____

5.2 HOW TO BE ALONE

1 VOCABULARY: Talking about influences

A **Write *N* for noun, *V* for verb, or *B* for words that can be either nouns or verbs.**

1 consequence N
2 stem from ___
3 influence ___
4 motivate ___
5 impact ___
6 trigger ___

7 result in ___
8 force ___
9 source ___
10 result in ___
11 implications ___

B (Circle) **the correct words and phrases to complete the paragraph.**

I used to be a truck driver, transporting food and other goods from one city to another. The job paid well, but working as a truck driver had a negative ¹*source /* (*impact*) on my life. The problem was the fact that I was alone for days at a time. Sometimes my trips lasted over a week. ²*The source / The consequence* of this was that I had trouble making and keeping friends. This ³*stemmed from / resulted in* not being home long enough to spend time with other people. When I did have a couple of days to spend at home, I was so tired from driving that I just wanted to sleep and relax. On my birthday last year, I realized that I didn't have anyone to spend my day with. That experience finally ⁴*motivated / impacted* me to change jobs. Now I deliver mail in my own city. My job change ⁵*has impacted / has triggered* my life in positive ways. I work regular hours and get off of work at 5:00, so I have time to hang out with friends. I also have more energy than I did when I was on the road all day. Another truck driver that I know is thinking about a job change. I'm hoping that my positive experience will ⁶*influence / stem from* him and encourage him to take that step like I did.

2 GRAMMAR: Reduced relative clauses

A **Read the reduced relative clauses and add a relative pronoun and the correct form of *be* to each one.**

1 People ^ *who are* uncomfortable being alone all day should not work as truck drivers.
2 Lighthouses, usually far from cities and towns, are lonesome places.
3 Working alone is a good solution for anyone in need of time to themselves.
4 Writers, able to make their own schedules, often find themselves working odd hours.
5 Swimming pool lifeguards, usually surrounded by other people, can't spend time talking to those people because they have to focus on watching swimmers.

B   **Combine the two sentences using a complete relative clause. Then cross out two words to form a reduced relative clause.**

1   Some people are happy being alone. These people enjoy being lighthouse keepers or truck drivers.

Some people, ~~who are~~ happy being alone, enjoy being lighthouse keepers or truck drivers.

2   Someone might be thinking about getting a job that requires solitude. They should consider it carefully before they make a decision.

_____

3   Solitude is a problem for some people. It isn't a problem for me.

_____

4   Some people are lonely because they work alone. They should get together with friends at least once a month.

_____

5   Is anyone able to go without speaking to someone for a whole week? I don't know anyone who can do that.

_____

6   I work in a remote area. The area is fifty miles away from the nearest town.

_____

3   GRAMMAR AND VOCABULARY

A   **Complete the sentences with words from the box and your own ideas. Use reduced relative clauses when possible.**

impact	result in	source	trigger

1   The _____ *root* _____ of my problem is the never-ending solitude _____ *required by my job* _____ .

2   Working alone would have a positive _____ on an individual _____

    _____ .

3   Working alone all day can _____ some people to create networks with other people

    _____ .

4   Working remotely can be very isolating and _____ feelings of loneliness for people

    _____ .

5   Solitude can _____ depression for people

    _____ .

1   LISTENING

A   🔊 **5.01**   **LISTEN FOR THE MAIN IDEA**   **Listen to the discussion. Then write answers to the questions.**

1   Where are the speakers?

2   What is Leah suggesting?

B   🔊 **5.01**   **LISTEN FOR DETAILS**   **Listen again and ⟨circle⟩ all the correct answers.**

1   Who likes the idea of working from home?

   a   Jack   **b**   Fatima   **c**   Jack and Martin   **d**   Jack and Fatima

2   Who can't concentrate in the office?

   a   Jack   **b**   Leah   **c**   Jack and Leah   **d**   Fatima and Martin

3   Who drives at least thirty minutes to get to work?

   a   Fatima   **b**   Jack and Martin   **c**   Fatima and Martin   **d**   Leah and Fatima

C   **DIFFERENTIATE FACTS AND OPINIONS**   **Read the excerpts from the meeting and write _O_ (opinion) or _F_ (fact).**

1   … other departments in this company have started allowing people to work from home a few days a week.   _F_

2   We thought that this might hurt productivity … ___

3   … employees in those departments have increased their productivity by 30%. ___

4   In the past twelve months, productivity in this department has steadily decreased. ___

5   … I really think that we need to make a change in our department … ___

6   Working from home sounds like a great solution to my problem. ___

7   I would be able to concentrate better at home. ___

8   Also, I live more than thirty minutes away from the office. ___

2   CRITICAL THINKING

A   **THINK CRITICALLY**   **Why do you think Leah thought letting people work from home would hurt productivity?**

3 SPEAKING

A **Which phrases fit in each sentence? Write them in the correct places in the chart.**

As a result of	Because of	Consequently,	Due to	For these reasons,
The outcomes of	Thanks to	That's why	The consequences of	

	… the change, productivity has increased.
	… we've decided to allow people to work from home.
	… this have been happier employees and higher productivity.

B **Imagine that your company has decided to let you work from home three days a week. List some possible effects of this change. Then use four of your ideas to complete the sentences.**

Possible Effects:

1 Due to this change, _____ .

2 One consequence of _____ .

3 Thanks to the fact that I can work from home _____ .

4 For these reasons, _____ .

REMOTE SUCCESS STORY

1 READING

A **PREDICT CONTENT** Look at the title of the article and the visual. What do you think the article is going to be about?

B **READ FOR MAIN IDEA** Read the article and (circle) the best summary of it.

a Lullabot, 100% remote from the very beginning, benefits from having a completely remote workforce.

b Lullabot, a website strategy, design and development company, has decided to allow all of its employees to begin working from home.

c Lullabot, a Rhode Island-based company, explains the advantages and disadvantages of having a remote workforce.

Lullabot

REMOTE FROM THE START

Lullabot, based in Providence, Rhode Island, is a website strategy, design, and development company. Unlike many companies, which move toward remote work after being fully established, Lullabot's employees have been working remotely since day one. Today, the company's employees are distributed all over the world.

As a result of having all their employees working remotely, the company has had to make communication with them a priority from the start. As Jared Ponchot, the company's creative director, points out, when a company begins to move from a traditional model to a remote model, it has to deal with certain difficulties. For example, the first employees to work remotely end up feeling out of the loop. This may be due to the fact

that the company continues to operate as if all of its workers are in-house, and doesn't make the changes needed to make sure that remote workers are included in everything. Owing to the fact that they began with a fully remote team, Lullabot has necessarily become adept at keeping everyone well-informed.

Being 100% remote has had positive effects on Lullabot's employees. Although Lullabot has standard business hours, the company's employees are able to have flexible schedules as long as they're meeting their work-related obligations. In addition, they have the time and the space to do their most creative work without unnecessary interruptions. All-in-all, Lullabot sounds like a great company to work for.

C **READ FOR DETAILS** Find three examples of cause-and-effect expressions in the article. What alternatives might you use if you were telling a friend the same information?

1 Example: _____

   Alternative: _____

2 Example: _____

   Alternative: _____

3 Example: _____

   Alternative: _____

2 CRITICAL THINKING

A **THINK CRITICALLY** What would you say the writer's attitude toward Lullabot is? Find two examples to support your opinion.

_____

3 WRITING

A **CREATE COHESION** Use participial phrases to connect the ideas and reduce the information to one sentence. Check your work by referring to the text above.

1 Lullabot began as a remote company. Lullabot's management has a lot of experience with remote workers.

   Having begun as a remote company, Lullabot's management has a lot of experience with remote workers.

2 Lullabot's employees can work wherever they want to. The employees can choose workspaces where they feel most comfortable.

   _____

3 Other companies see Lullabot as a successful remote company. Lullabot is a good model for other companies that want to go remote.

   _____

B Use the information in the box to write a profile of a company. Include at least two introductory participle phrases and two phrases to show cause and effect.

> MobileApp Company—App Designer and Developer
> - Everyone works remotely on Wednesday through Friday.
> - Employees are more productive at home.
> - No commuting means employees are less stressed.
> - Employees are more creative when they're not stressed.
> - The company is considering becoming 100% remote.

_____

_____

_____

_____

_____

_____

CHECK AND REVIEW

Read the statements. Can you do these things?

UNIT 5	Mark the boxes. ☑ I can do it. ? I am not sure.		If you are not sure, go back to these pages in the Student's Book.
	I can …		
VOCABULARY	☐ describe remote places.		page 44
	☐ talk about influences.		page 46
GRAMMAR	☐ use participle phrases in initial position.		page 45
	☐ use reduced relative clauses.		page 47
LISTENING AND SPEAKING SKILLS	☐ differentiate facts and opinions in a discussion.		page 48
	☐ discuss the effects of working remotely.		page 49
READING AND WRITING SKILLS	☐ analyze the content of an article.		page 50
	☐ write a company profile.		page 51

6.1 THE SURPRISE BUSINESS

1 VOCABULARY: Using adverbs to add attitude

A Match the words with their meanings.

1 truly _____
2 as expected _____
3 clearly _____ , _____
4 very _____ , _____

a visibly
b utterly
c understandably
d genuinely
e immensely
f noticeably

B Complete the story with the words from the box.

anxious	calm	helpful
popular	shaken	~~shocked~~
surprised	thrilled	unusual
upset		

Marta was utterly [1] _____shocked_____ when her best friend, Lisa, gave her a gift certificate for a helicopter ride for her birthday. Lisa had bought the certificate from an immensely [2] _____ company that was known to give helicopter rides to celebrities. It was a highly [3] _____ gift, just like all of Lisa's birthday presents.

Marta looked visibly [4] _____ by the idea of going up in a helicopter. Lisa was genuinely [5] _____ to see Marta's reaction to her gift. What Lisa didn't know was that Marta was deeply [6] _____ about flying. She was understandably [7] _____ that she had given Marta a gift that she didn't want. However, she stayed remarkably [8] _____ , even though she felt terrible.

Lisa called the helicopter company and asked if she could get a refund. The person she talked to was incredibly [9] _____ and gave her a full refund. Lisa used the money to buy her friend a day at the spa instead. Marta was noticeably [10] _____ by the new gift, and the two friends spent a nice, relaxing day at the spa with both feet firmly on the ground.

2 GRAMMAR: Clefts

A Check (✓) the correct sentences. Then correct the mistakes in the incorrect sentences.

1 The thing that I most try to avoid it is spiders. ☐
2 What I didn't expect was to have lunch with my favorite actor. ☐
3 What I hate most it is being surprised. ☐
4 The reason why that surprises scare me. ☐
5 It wasn't until it was all over that I was able to calm down. ☐
6 The gifts that I enjoy most the ones that I never expected. ☐

B **Complete the sentences. Match 1–8 with a–h.**

1 What I didn't expect was   f
2 The thing I love most is
3 The reason why I'm late is
4 What I love about traveling is
5 It wasn't until I got home
6 The place I most want to visit is
7 What I love most about my job is
8 What I never expected was

a taking walks on the beach.
b Istanbul, Turkey.
c meeting new people in new places.
d that I would enjoy living in a big city.
e that I realized that I had lost my scarf.
f that we'd spend the day on a boat.
g that my car broke down.
h the people that I work with.

<h1>3   GRAMMAR AND VOCABULARY</h1>

A **Complete the sentences to make them true for you.**

1 What makes me understandably upset is when someone

2 The thing that makes me most deeply anxious is when I have to

3 My best friend was noticeably thrilled when

4 The person I find most helpful is
   because

5 One thing that makes me remarkably calm is

6 The time I was utterly shocked was

7 The most immensely popular place I've ever been to is

8 The last time I was genuinely surprised was

THE MIRACLE ON ICE

1 VOCABULARY: Using the prefixes *under-* and *over-*

A **Look at the clues and complete the crossword.**

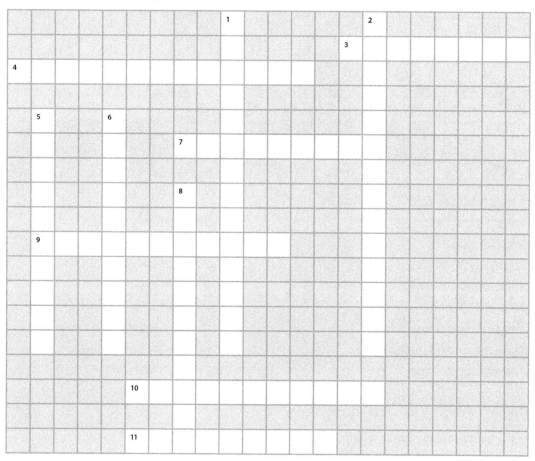

Across

3 the person or team is considered to be the weakest and the least likely to win a competition

4 feeling too sure about yourself

7 thought to be better than it is

9 feeling like you have too much to deal with

10 costing less than something is worth

11 not getting enough money for your work

Down

1 having thought that someone has less power or ability than they have

2 not advanced as much as something should be

5 made to work too much

6 costing more than something is worth

8 having too many people in one place

B **Complete each sentence with a word from exercise 1A. Change the prefix if necessary.**

1 This movie is _____. It's not as good as everyone says it is.

2 I have so much work to do. I'm feeling _____.

3 We really _____ how many people were going to be at this party. We didn't make enough food!

4 You should charge more for your paintings. I think they're _____.

5 I think I'm _____. I just found out that other people in this company are making a lot more money than I am.

2 GRAMMAR: Question words with -ever

A **Complete the sentences. Match 1–6 with a–f.**

1 You should do   _b_   a   it's far from here.

2 We can leave   ___   b   whatever you want.

3 I'll get the money for school   ___   c   make sure you tell him the news.

4 Wherever he lives,   ___   d   didn't leave a message.

5 However you contact him,   ___   e   whenever you're ready.

6 Whoever called you   ___   f   however I can.

B **Complete each sentence with the correct question word from the box.**

however	whatever	whenever	wherever	whichever	whoever

1 I see that woman _____ I go! She's everywhere!

2 I don't think you should do it. It's a bad idea _____ you look at it.

3 Look at that guy over there. _____ he is, he looks just like your brother.

4 Are you still trying to decide which school to go to? _____ school you choose, I'm sure you'll enjoy college.

5 I've applied to ten different jobs in the last month. _____ I do, I just can't get a job!

6 I can't ride in the back of the car. _____ I do, I get sick.

3 GRAMMAR AND VOCABULARY

A **Complete the conversations with words from the box and question words with -ever.**

overcrowded	overpriced	overrated	~~underestimated~~

1 **A** I just watched a movie called *Miracle on Ice*. I guess everyone really _underestimated_ Team USA's abilities.

   B ___However you look at it___ , it was an amazing moment in sports history.

2 **A** I'm not sure which car to buy. This car is _____ , but it's in really good condition. The other car needs some work, but the price is great.

   B _____ , make sure you get good insurance.

3 **A** We went to the beach today, and it was really _____ . We couldn't find a place to sit.

   B _____ , there are always too many people there.

4 **A** Are you sure you want to go to this restaurant? I think it might be _____ . John went there last week and said it's not as good as we've heard.

   B I'll do _____ you want. We can go somewhere else if you want.

1 LISTENING

A 🔊 **6.01** **LISTEN FOR MAIN POINTS** **Listen to a podcast episode about the Maker Movement. Circle the two main points.**

a Lila Marcus makes jewelry and is a ceramics artist.

b Makers are people who make things, such as clothing, furniture, and jewelry, instead of buying things.

c Buying handmade goods is better for the economy than buying things from corporate-owned stores.

d Social media and websites are full of information about how to make things instead of buying them.

e An increasing number of people are learning to make things themselves.

B 🔊 **6.01** **LISTEN FOR DETAILS** **Listen again. Write *T* (true) or *F* (false). Correct the false statements.**

1 Makers ~~don't~~ use tools. _F_

2 The important thing for makers is that they make handmade goods. ___

3 The Maker Movement started a few years ago. ___

4 It was immediately obvious that the Maker Movement was starting. ___

5 Lila talks about websites that teach you how to make things yourself. ___

6 Some makers are starting their own businesses, but they're not successful. ___

7 Lila thinks that people stopped making things because they could buy better products in stores. ___

8 Lila believes that the Maker Movement is happening because makers want to learn skills that people had in the past. ___

C 🔊 **6.02** **Listen to the sentences and circle the words that you hear.**

1 really   actually   (simply)

2 actually   really   even

3 even   simply   actually

4 simply   even   really

5 didn't know   did know   do know

6 exactly right totally obsessed genuinely delighted

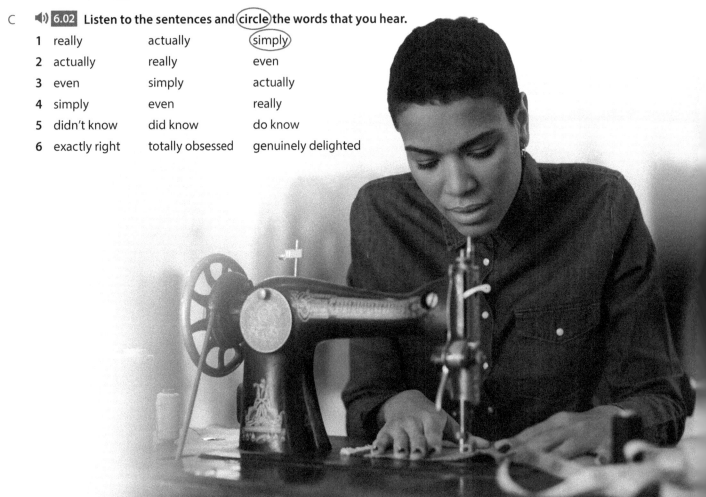

2 SPEAKING

A Circle the correct word or phrase to complete each sentence.

Matthew So, Lila, tell me about what you like to make.

Lila Well, I've been a maker for a long time. I design and sew my own clothes. I make jewelry, and I make ceramic pieces, like plates, bowls, and mugs. I ¹*even / simply* made my own kitchen table.

Matthew Wow, that must have been challenging.

Lila It ²*even / really* was.

Matthew You've been able to make a successful business out of your crafts, right?

Lila Yes, that's right. I sell my jewelry online. It wasn't ³*immediately clear / exactly right* to me at first which of my crafts I should sell. However, ⁴*what I enjoyed making most was / what I enjoyed making most were* jewelry, so I decided to go with that.

Matthew Were you successful right away?

Lila No, I wasn't. ⁵*Even / Actually*, for the first few months, I didn't sell anything at all. I started to worry, but then a friend of mine helped me redesign my website and I started an Instagram account for my jewelry. I didn't know if it was going to work, but then it ⁶*does / did* help a lot. I was ⁷*extremely anxious / genuinely thrilled* when that happened.

B Read the information in the box about Eli, a maker who makes furniture. Then complete the interview between Matthew and Eli. Use at least four words or phrases for adding emphasis.

> makes tables, chairs, cabinets, sofas
> sells furniture online and in stores
> shocked when people started buying his furniture
>
> is successful
> was successful right away
> advice: Don't give up!

Matthew Tell me about what you like to make, Eli.

Eli _____

_____

Matthew Have you been able to create a successful business?

Eli _____

_____

Matthew Was your business immediately successful?

Eli _____

_____

Matthew What are some tips you would give to a maker who wants to start a business?

Eli _____

_____

1 READING

A **PREDICT CONTENT** Look at the headlines. Match each headline to the correct topic.

1 The Face of Fear ____   a why we enjoy being scared

2 Fear for Fun ____   b how our bodies react to fear

3 Overcoming Fear ____   c what we look like when we're scared

4 Fight or Flight Response ____   d how to deal with our fears

B **READ FOR MAIN IDEAS** Read the stories and write the correct headline for each one. Use two of the headlines from exercise 1A.

A _____

Imagine that you're sitting in your dark living room watching a scary movie. The main character hears a noise in the basement. She decides to go down to see what it is. As a viewer, you know that there's a monster in the basement and the main character shouldn't go downstairs. You also know that at some point soon, the monster is going to jump out at the main character. Still, even though you're expecting it, you jump. What does your face look like at this moment? If you were genuinely scared, your eyes would be wide and your mouth open. Why does this happen? Scientist Charles Darwin had an explanation. He found that when we are scared, we instinctively tighten our muscles, even the muscles in our face. This is so we are ready to defend ourselves or run away if we have to. When we are truly scared, we can't avoid tightening these muscles, and inevitably, we make the face of fear.

B _____

When you feel scared, whether it's for a moment when someone jumps out at you from behind a door, or for several minutes while you wonder if the noise you hear outside is a burglar or just your neighbor's cat, your body changes in certain ways. Some of these changes are noticeable. Your heart beats faster, your breathing rate increases, and your face might become flushed or get very pale. Other changes are not visible. Your blood vessels become wider, your digestion slows down or might even stop, and your hearing and vision become very focused. All of these changes are part of your fight or flight response to fear, and they help you fight off an attacker or get away as fast as you can. For example, wider blood vessels allow more blood to get to your muscles so they are stronger. Your digestion slows down because your body needs all its energy to deal with the current threat. And your hearing and vision change so you can locate a threat more easily.

2 CRITICAL THINKING

A **THINK CRITICALLY** How do you think the fight or flight response might have helped humans 15,000 years ago? How might it not be as useful to us now?

_____

_____

_____

3 WRITING

A Read this summary of one of the topics below based on information from the two texts in exercise 1B. Which topic is it summarizing? Circle the topic.

why we like to be scared   why fear makes us react in certain ways

All of the changes that happen in our bodies when we're afraid help us to deal with the threat we are facing. Our physical reactions help us become stronger so we can locate a threat, fight against it, or run away from it.

B Write a short summary of the topic that wasn't summarized in exercise 3A.

_____

_____

_____

_____

_____

_____

_____

CHECK AND REVIEW

Read the statements. Can you do these things?

UNIT 6	Mark the boxes. ☑ I can do it. ? I am not sure. I can ...	If you are not sure, go back to these pages in the Student's Book.
VOCABULARY	☐ use adverbs to add attitude.	page 54
	☐ use the prefixes *under-* and *over-*.	page 56
GRAMMAR	☐ use clefts.	page 55
	☐ use question words with *-ever*.	page 57
LISTENING AND SPEAKING SKILLS	☐ listen for details in a podcast.	page 58
	☐ use phrases to add emphasis.	page 59
READING AND WRITING SKILLS	☐ read two stories and identify the main focus.	page 60
	☐ write a short summary of a topic.	page 61

UNIT **7** ROOTS

7.1 IT'S IN THE BLOOD

1 VOCABULARY: Talking about ancestry

A **Match the words with the definitions.**

1	adopt	*b*	a	the study of the history of a person's family
2	adoption		b	to legally make someone else's child part of your own family
3	adoptive		c	relating to the way traits are passed from parents to children
4	ancestral		d	relating to a family member from any time in the past
5	ancestor		e	the fact of belonging to a cultural or national group
6	ancestry		f	to be born with a family member's characteristics
7	ethnic		g	the process of getting legal permission to raise someone's child
8	ethnicity		h	relating to cultural or national origins
9	genealogy		i	traditions and other features belonging to a culture
10	genes		j	a member of your family from any time in the past
11	genetic		k	the long line of people who came before you
12	hereditary		l	the characteristics of a person inherited from parents
13	heritage		m	related, especially as parents of someone, through adoption
14	inherit		n	relating to the qualities we inherit from our ancestors

B **Check (✓) the correct sentences. Then correct the mistakes in the incorrect sentences.**

1 I sent off a DNA sample to find out about my ~~genealogy~~ *genetic* history. ☐

2 Before I sent it, I didn't know much about my ethnic. ☐

3 I'm adopted, and I don't know much about my biological parents. ☐

4 My adoption parents never met my biological parents. ☐

5 I found out that most of my ancestors were from Mongolia. ☐

6 Now I'm trying to learn as much as possible about my Mongolian hereditary. ☐

7 Looking at pictures of people from Mongolia, I can see that I probably inherited
a lot of my features from my Mongolian ancestors. ☐

2 GRAMMAR: Negative and limiting adverbials

A <u>Underline</u> the negative and limiting adverbials.

1 Never had I imagined that I might be 23% Eastern European.

2 Only when I asked my father did I find out that his grandparents
were from Russia.

3 Not until I had children did I become interested in genealogy.

4 Only when I had discovered more about my genetic makeup did
I want to find out who my ancestors were.

5 Little did I know my great grandparents were from Tokyo.

B **Put the words in the correct order to make sentences. Add a form of *do* when necessary.**

1 I would / South America / to find / be able / relatives / in / never / I / think

   Never did I think I would be able to find relatives in South America.

2 from my / I / realize / little / grandmother / I inherited / my freckles

   _____

3 would / had an aunt / never / towns away / guessed / that I / I have / living two

   _____

4 tell me / my mother / only when / I asked / that I'm / part Irish

   _____

5 I sent in / a DNA sample / Asian ancestry / not until / I know / that I have

   _____

6 without using / have found / no way / my cousins / a DNA ancestry kit / would / I

   _____

C **Circle the correct words and phrases to complete the sentences.**

1 *Not until / Never* would I have imagined that I was related to a famous singer.

2 *Little / Not until* I met my grandfather did I know who I inherited my height from.

3 *Little / Only* did I know I'm not actually Spanish at all.

4 *Only when / Not until* my friend suggested getting a DNA test did I even consider it.

5 *Not until / No way* would I have considered getting a DNA test before my friend did his.

3 GRAMMAR AND VOCABULARY

A **Complete the stories with the words in parentheses and your own ideas.**

1 My whole life I thought I was 100% Italian. Imagine my shock when I found some relatives online and found out that my mother's great grandparents were Chinese! No way (ancestors)

   _____ .

2 I grew up learning all about Italian culture. I didn't know anything about Chinese culture. Not until (heritage)

   _____ .

3 My mother didn't believe me when I told her about what I had discovered, so I showed her the genealogy record that my relatives sent me. Only when (ancestry)

   _____ .

4 I did some more research and found out that we also have roots in Sweden. We always wondered who my little brother inherited his blond hair and blue eyes from. Little (genes)

   _____ .

7.2 A VERY SPECIAL OCCASION

1 VOCABULARY: Talking about customs and traditions

A **Complete the chart with the words in the box.**

festivities	honor (our grandmother)	keep alive	mark (the occasion)
observe	pay tribute to	(this) practice	rites
ritual	significance	signify	symbolize

Nouns	Verbs

B **Circle the correct words to complete the story.**

Every year, my family gets together to ¹*honor / observe* the holiday of *Chuseok*, a Korean harvest celebration. The ²*festivities / practices* take place during the eighth month of the lunar year when there's a full moon.

We always prepare a lot of delicious foods for *Chuseok*. The abundance of food ³*signifies / honors* a good harvest. One of these foods is *seongpyeon*, a type of rice cake. It is white, shaped like a half circle, and filled with things like sesame seeds or pine nuts. Because of its shape, it ⁴*marks / symbolizes* the moon.

Ancestors are also an important part of *Chuseok*. First, we have a memorial service at home. This ⁵*significance / ritual* usually takes place in the morning. Then we visit our ancestors' graves later in the day to *observe / honor* them.

My family and I participate in Chuseok because we really enjoy it, but more importantly, we do it because we want to help ⁶*keep / mark* these traditions ⁷*significant / alive*.

2 GRAMMAR: Fronting adverbials

A **Complete the sentences. Match 1–5 with a–e.**

1 On the table   *d*   a people are talking and having fun.
2 From the kitchen   ___   b float sounds of raindrops falling.
3 Around the house   ___   c is bread baking to a golden-brown color.
4 Through the window   ___   d lay plates full of traditional foods.
5 In the oven   ___   e come sounds of cooking and laughing.

52

B **Check (✓) the correct sentences. Then correct the mistakes in the incorrect sentences.**

                   people cook

1 In the kitchen ~~cook people~~ traditional foods. ☐

2 Throughout the house we put up decorations. ☐

3 From the living room coming the sounds of the television. ☐

4 On the walls hang we pictures of our ancestors. ☐

5 From the backyard float the sounds of children playing. ☐

C **Bring the adverbials in bold to the front of each sentence. Make any changes to word order that are needed.**

1 The sound of a fire crackling comes **from the fireplace**.

    From the fireplace comes the sound of a fire crackling.

2 Adults and children are hanging decorations **around the house**.

3 Sounds of music and chatter come **from the kitchen**.

4 Delicious scents of cooking waft **throughout the house**.

5 Traditional dishes are **in the oven** roasting.

6 A beautiful vase of flowers sits **on the table**.

3 GRAMMAR AND VOCABULARY

A **Think about a celebration or event. Complete the sentences with your own ideas. Use words from the box in at least three of your sentences.**

rites	keep alive	observe	mark	festivities	ritual
significance	honor	symbolize	pay tribute to	practice	signify

1 In the kitchen _____ .

2 On the table _____ .

3 From the living room _____ .

4 Through the kitchen door _____ .

5 Around the house _____ .

7.3 THE STORY OF A RETURNEE

1 LISTENING

A 🔊 **7.01** **LISTEN FOR ATTITUDE** How did the following things affect Elsa? Match each part of her experience with the correct attitude.

1	speaking German ___	**a**	overwhelmed
2	meeting all her relatives ___	**b**	happy
3	staying at her aunt's house ___	**c**	anxious

B 🔊 **7.01** **DEDUCE MEANING** Look at the words and phrases from the conversation. What do they mean? Listen again and use context clues to help you figure out the meanings.

1 tongue-tied
  a talking too much **b** unable to speak **c** having a sore throat

2 gibberish
  a meaningful words **b** a specific language **c** words that don't make sense

3 keeping everyone straight
  a remembering who is who **b** having people stand in line **c** being very serious with people

4 fried
  a overcooked **b** energetic **c** exhausted

5 anticipated
  a excited **b** expected **c** wondered

6 hit it off
  a got to know each other **b** got into a fight **c** got along well

C 🔊 **7.01** **LISTEN FOR DETAILS** Listen again and read the statements about Elsa. Write *T* (true) or *F* (false).

1 She was nervous before she got to Germany. ___
2 She went to Germany alone. ___
3 She doesn't speak any German. ___
4 She met over 100 people at the reunion. ___
5 She remembers everyone's name. ___
6 She stayed at her grandparents' house. ___
7 She enjoyed meeting two of her cousins. ___
8 Her cousins are almost the same age as she is. ___
9 She is going to visit her cousins again next summer. ___
10 Her mother visits her sister in Germany once a year. ___

2 CRITICAL THINKING

A **THINK CRITICALLY** What do you think Elsa learned from having gone to her family reunion in Germany?

_____

_____

3 SPEAKING

A **Read the expressions. Write *C* (commenting on your own story), *E* (expressing an opinion), or *R* (responding to someone else's story).**

1 I can see how it would be strange. _____
2 To tell you the truth, … _____
3 How did you handle that? _____

4 It's difficult to say why, exactly. _____
5 It's hard to describe. _____
6 Don't get me wrong, … _____

B **Put the conversation in the correct order.**

_____ **Elsa** That was the weirdest part! I look so much like all these people I'd never met before.

_1_ **Max** How was the food at the reunion? Was it as good as your mom's?

_____ **Elsa** To tell you the truth, it helped me feel like part of the family.

_____ **Max** I think I can understand that. So, did you see a family resemblance between you and any of your relatives?

_____ **Elsa** I have to admit, it was even better than my mom's. It was delicious. I got some recipes from my aunt. I'll make one of the dishes for you.

_____ **Elsa** It was beautiful. It's difficult to put into words, but I really felt the history of the place. There are so many old buildings there. In some places, I felt like I'd stepped back in time, if you know what I mean.

_____ **Max** I can see how that would be strange. Did it make you feel uncomfortable?

_____ **Max** I can't wait to try it. How did you like Germany in general?

C **Imagine that you took a trip like Elsa's. Complete the conversation with your own ideas.**

A How was your trip to _____ ?

B To tell you the truth, _____ .

A It must have been pretty overwhelming. Did you like the food?

B That was the best part! _____ .

A That sounds great. Did you enjoy meeting your family members?

B Well, I was really nervous. It's difficult to say why exactly, but _____ .

55

1 READING

A **READ THE MAIN IDEA** Read the article below. Then (circle) the main idea.

a It is impossible for one person to successfully create a new language.

b It is important to preserve languages that are disappearing.

c Constructed languages might prove that language affects thought.

B **READ FOR ATTITUDE** Read the article again. Is the writer emotionally engaged? Why do you think so?

What Can We Learn from Constructed Languages?

One argument for saving disappearing languages is the idea that when we lose a language, we lose a way of thinking. Can language affect, or even control, the way we think? Examining constructed languages – those created by a single person or group of people – shows us that our thoughts might be limited by the words we use.

Many people may be familiar with languages invented for TV shows, such as *Star Trek* (Klingon) and *Game of Thrones* (Dothraki). However, hundreds of languages have been constructed. One of these is Newspeak, which was invented by author George Orwell for his novel *1984*. In the novel, the rulers of Oceania create Newspeak, based on English, in order to control their citizens. One way that they achieve this is by limiting vocabulary. With a greatly reduced vocabulary, citizens don't have the words to express complex thoughts, and the rulers hope this will stop them from actually *having* complex thoughts.

Another language that attempts to affect thought is E-Prime. Also based on English, E-Prime has only one special rule – it doesn't include any form of the verb *be*. Because the verb *be* is used so frequently in English, this simple change requires speakers to be more creative and more precise with their speech. For example, instead of saying "That's a terrible idea," an E-Prime speaker has to say something like, "I don't think that idea will work."

Newspeak and E-Prime are two examples of languages that were created with the goal of influencing thought and expression. One attempts to limit thought and the other tries to expand it. Would they have influenced people's thoughts if they were actually widely spoken? Those who argue that thought creates language might say no. However, I believe that it's the other way around—language creates thought.

2 CRITICAL THINKING

A **THINK CRITICALLY** Do you agree with the writer's conclusion? Why or why not?

_____

_____

_____

_____

_____

_____

_____

3 WRITING

A **Read the summary of the text. Has the writer captured the main idea and argument correctly? <u>Underline</u> any incorrect information. Is there any key information missing?**

The constructed languages Newspeak and E-Prime show us that language can affect thought. Newspeak does this by restricting vocabulary. In addition, it restricts the use of the verb *be* so that speakers have to be creative in order to express their ideas. E-Prime, which is based on English, aims to make speakers and writers use more precise language, thereby influencing the way they think. Some say that thought influences language. However, Newspeak and E-Prime show us that language might, in fact, control thought.

B **Rewrite the end of the summary in exercise 3A using one of the parallel structures below.**

Some argue that … but the author disagrees, saying …

While some say … , the author feels …

Many claim that … However, the author maintains that …

C **Rewrite the summary in exercise 3A. Make sure that it captures the main idea and argument correctly and that there's no key information missing.**

CHECK AND REVIEW

Read the statements. Can you do these things?

UNIT 7	Mark the boxes. ✔ I can do it. ? I am not sure.	If you are not sure, go back to these pages in the Student's Book.
	I can …	
VOCABULARY	☐ talk about ancestry.	page 66
	☐ talk about customs and traditions.	page 68
GRAMMAR	☐ use negative and limiting adverbials.	page 67
	☐ use fronting adverbials.	page 69
LISTENING AND SPEAKING SKILLS	☐ listen to a podcast and deduce meaning from context clues.	page 70
	☐ comment on my own story, express an opinion, and respond to someone else's story.	page 71
READING AND WRITING SKILLS	☐ identify bias in an article.	page 73
	☐ write a summary with a concluding statement.	page 73

1 VOCABULARY: Talking about attention and distraction

A Complete the chart with the correct form of each word.

Nouns	Verbs
concentration	
	distract
focus	
	interrupt

B Complete the phrases with the words in the box.

~~distracted~~   distractions   focus   focused   interrupted

1 be / get _____ *distracted* _____
2 be / get _____
3 get / stay _____
4 lose _____
5 avoid _____

C Complete the sentences with words from exercise 1A. Include the words *by* and *on* when necessary. For some items, more than one answer may be possible.

1 It's hard to get back to work after a(n) _____ *interruption* _____ .
2 I can't study in coffee shops because I get _____ by the people around me.
3 I try not to _____ people when they're busy working.
4 Do you find it difficult to _____ on work when people are talking?
5 I avoid _____ by closing my office door.

2 GRAMMAR: Phrases with *get*

A Check (✓) the correct sentences. Then correct the mistakes in the incorrect sentences.

1 It's hard for me to get ~~focus~~ *focused* in a noisy room. ☐
2 The article got me wondered about my own attention span. ☐
3 I'm getting annoyed by all the distractions. ☐
4 I can't get my work finish in this environment. ☐
5 The conversation got thinking about the distractions I deal with every day. ☐
6 I get distracted easily. ☐
7 I'm getting exhaust by all the demands on my attention. ☐
8 Can you help me have this window open? ☐

B **Write sentences using the cues in parentheses.**

1 (I can't / get / anything / do / today)

I can't get anything done today.

2 (your comment yesterday / get / me / think / about my workspace)

3 (right now/ my patience / get / eat away /by constant interruptions)

4 (it's easy / get / distract / around here)

5 (How can you / get / focus / with all these distractions)

6 (yesterday's meeting / get / us / talk / about the future of the company)

3 GRAMMAR AND VOCABULARY

A **Complete the sentences with your own ideas.**

1 My ability to concentrate is getting _____ .

2 If I pay attention to all the distractions around me, I can't get _____ .

3 This discussion on ways to improve concentration got _____ .

4 When I have trouble focusing, I get _____ .

1 VOCABULARY: Expressions with *get*

A **Match the phrases with the definitions.**

get …

1	accustomed to something	h	**a** to become irritated and impatient
2	at	___	**b** to have trouble finding a destination
3	attached to something	___	**c** to imply something
4	blown away by something	___	**d** to be amazed by something
5	complicated	___	**e** to do something correctly
6	frustrated	___	**f** to throw something away
7	lost	___	**g** to receive permission to do something
8	rid of something	___	**h** to get used to something
9	something right	___	**i** to develop a liking for something
10	something straight	___	**j** to become problematic or complex
11	the go-ahead	___	**k** to understand something thoroughly

B **Circle the correct words to complete the conversations.**

1 **A** What happened? You were supposed to be here twenty minutes ago.

  B Sorry, I missed the turn for your street and got *the go-ahead /* *lost*. I had to ask someone for directions.

2 **A** It must be difficult to go from sales associate to manager.

  B No, it's great. I'm really getting *accustomed to / frustrated* managing the department.

3 **A** I got *rid of / at* all my old clothes last weekend.

  B I have to do that, too. I don't wear most of the things in my closet.

4 **A** Let me get *this right / this straight*. Are you saying that you can speak seven languages?

  B Yes, I can!

5 **A** You don't seem excited about moving. I think you're going to love London.

  B I am excited, but I'm sad about leaving this apartment. I've lived here for three years, and I've really gotten *blown away by / attached to* it.

6 **A** Have you made the restaurant reservation for Callie's birthday dinner yet?

  B No, I'm waiting to get *it right / the go-ahead* from Callie.

C **THINK CRITICALLY** **Think of a time you trusted your instincts. What happened? Were you right or wrong?**

_____

_____

_____

_____

2 GRAMMAR: Phrases with *as*

A **Put the words in the correct order to form sentences with *as* phrases.**

1 trust yourself / as my / says, / someone else / before / you trust / grandmother

_____

2 more accurate / explains / in his book, / instinct / as Gladwell / can be / than careful consideration

_____

3 instincts all / to follow / it can / the time / as / be difficult / we all know, / your

_____

4 make decisions / half of / say they / as / can be seen / based on instincts / in the graph, / the employees

_____

5 their instincts / as / follow / we / can infer / most participants / from the study,

_____

B **Complete the sentences with phrases from the box.**

all attest	can be	explains	inferred	point out

1 As _____ seen in the report, it takes about 23 minutes to get back to a task after an interruption.

2 As the article _____, constant interruptions increase workers' stress.

3 As the researchers _____, the average office worker switches tasks approximately every five minutes.

4 As we can _____, it's not possible to concentrate on a difficult task when we're interrupted every few minutes.

5 As can be _____ from the chart, interruptions take up a large amount of an employee's workday.

3 GRAMMAR AND VOCABULARY

A **Complete the sentences with your own ideas and expressions from the box.**

get accustomed to	get attached to	get blown away by	get complicated
get frustrated	get lost	get rid of	get something right

1 As my mother always says, _____.

2 As you can imagine, _____.

3 As my teacher points out, _____.

4 As you can see, _____.

5 As we can all attest, _____.

IT'S THE APP YOU NEED

1 LISTENING

A 🔊 8.01 **LISTEN FOR MAIN POINTS** Listen to the conversation. What kind of device are Tina and Yuri discussing?

a one that improves sleep

b one that monitors apps that most distract you

c one that improves concentration

B 🔊 8.01 **LISTEN FOR DETAILS** Listen again and write answers to the questions.

1 What types of disruptions did Yuri have at work?

2 What do the headsets enable users to do?

3 What do the headsets do when a user gets distracted?

4 What is the whole point of the headsets?

5 Why does the app keep a record of a user's concentration patterns?

6 Why does the app play music?

C 🔊 8.02 Listen to the sentences and circle the words that you hear.

1 allow   enable   aim
2 offer   prefer   opportunity
3 goal   bottom   point
4 line   aim   miss
5 market   aim   goals

2 CRITICAL THINKING

A **THINK CRITICALLY** Think of three other ways that Yuri can avoid the kinds of distractions she had at work.

1 _____

2 _____

3 _____

3 SPEAKING

A **Complete the sentences with the phrases from the box.**

bottom line	enables users	goal is
great opportunity	miss out	on the market

1 The app _____ to keep track of tasks.

2 No other app _____ offers as many features.

3 Our _____ to help users get organized.

4 This is a _____ to try the app for free.

5 The _____ is that this is the best organizing app available.

6 You won't want to _____ on this excellent app.

B **Think of a useful device that you use on a regular basis. Then complete the sentences below to create an advertisement for the device.**

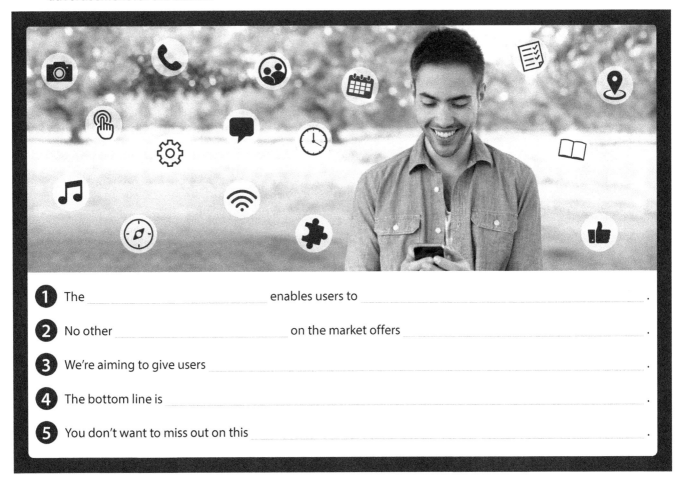

1 The _____ enables users to _____ .

2 No other _____ on the market offers _____ .

3 We're aiming to give users _____ .

4 The bottom line is _____ .

5 You don't want to miss out on this _____ .

1 READING

A **Read the article. Write the subheads above the correct paragraphs. You will use only three of the subheads.**

Sit Down and Summarize	Share Your Knowledge
Speed Up Your Reading	Sleep on It
Take Breaks	Write It, Don't Type It

TIPS FOR BECOMING A QUICK LEARNER

Learning something new can be time consuming, but effectively retaining what you learn, without having to review it multiple times, can shorten the time you spend learning a new skill. Follow these tips for retaining information and learning more quickly.

1 _____

Pay attention to new information as if you were going to have to teach it to someone else. Approaching new information from a teacher's point of view can help you focus on key points and organize the information into manageable portions even when you are hearing the information for the first time. After you've heard or read the information once, teach it to someone else. That helps you retain what you've learned.

2 _____

After learning something new, get a good night's sleep. While you sleep, your brain activity doesn't stop. In fact, some brain functions thrive on sleep. For example, research shows that sleep helps the hippocampus, the part of the brain devoted to memory, form long-term memories. Storing information in your long-term memory means you're turning new information into knowledge.

3 _____

It may be tempting to type your notes on a laptop or tablet, particularly because most of us type faster than we write. However, research reveals that writing things by hand is far superior to typing when it comes to information retention. One reason for this is that most people can't write fast enough to write down every word that someone says. Because of this, we have to process the information, making decisions about what is important and what isn't as we take notes.

B **EVALUATE INFORMATION** Complete the chart with information from the article.

	Tip 1	Tip 2	Tip 3
How does following this tip help you learn more quickly?			

2 CRITICAL THINKING

A **THINK CRITICALLY** Which tip do you think is most useful for you? Why?

_____

_____

_____

_____

3 WRITING

A Choose the best phrases for slides based on the article.

Opening slide:

1 a Learn Quickly

   b You Can Become a Quick Learner

2 a These tips will help you learn faster

   b Three tips to speed up your learning

Tip 1:

3 a Learn like a teacher

   b Try to learn as if you were a teacher

4 a Focus on key points, retain information

   b Learning like a teacher helps you focus on and remember the important points

B Create presentation slides about Tips 2 and 3 of the article.

Tip 2	Tip 3

CHECK AND REVIEW

Read the statements. Can you do these things?

UNIT 8	Mark the boxes. ☑ I can do it. ? I am not sure.	If you are not sure, go back to these pages in the Student's Book.
	I can ...	
VOCABULARY	☐ talk about attention and distraction.	page 76
	☐ use expressions with _get_.	page 78
GRAMMAR	☐ use phrases with _get_.	page 77
	☐ use phrases with _as_.	page 79
LISTENING AND SPEAKING SKILLS	☐ listen for details in a conversation.	page 80
	☐ use phrases to speak persuasively about a product.	page 81
READING AND WRITING SKILLS	☐ analyze information in an article.	page 82
	☐ write presentation slides based on an article.	page 83

1 VOCABULARY: Discussing health issues

A Complete the phrases with words from the box. If a word is not part of a phrase, write an *X* on the line.

cardiovascular	cholesterol	internal
pain	pressure	sedentary
side	system	

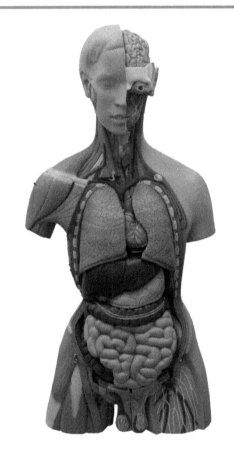

1 _____ effects

2 blood _____

3 posture _____

4 _____ lifestyle

5 immune _____

6 digestion _____

7 joints _____

8 _____ organs

9 _____ disease

10 _____ levels

11 chronic _____

12 circulation _____

B Write the correct word or phrase from exercise 1A next to each definition.

1 _____ body parts, such as the lungs and the heart, that are inside the body

2 _____ a network of cells and tissues that fight infection and disease in the body

3 _____ the movement of blood inside the body

4 _____ a way of living involving little or no physical activity

5 _____ an illness of the heart and blood vessels

6 _____ a constant ache

7 _____ the body's ability to process food

8 _____ measures of the fatty substance that is found in the blood

9 _____ the force at which the blood moves through the body

10 _____ unwanted results of something

11 _____ places in the body where two bones come together

12 _____ the way that someone holds their body when standing, sitting, or walking

2 GRAMMAR: Referencing

A Write *P* for pronoun, *PA* for possessive adjective, or *AV* for auxiliary verb next to each word.

1 their ____   3 this ____   5 does ____

2 were ____   4 they ____   6 its ____

B (Circle) the correct words and phrases to complete the paragraphs.

Do you eat healthy food and exercise regularly in order to have a healthy lifestyle? Even if you ¹*do / have / are*, there is one important aspect of your health that you might not think about—your posture. Poor posture makes your body work harder than it needs to, and ²*you / they / this* can result in serious consequences for the body, such as back pain and muscle aches. Good posture, on the other hand, allows you to use your muscles efficiently and helps ensure that ³*it / they / their* remain healthy as you grow older.

If you feel that you have bad posture, there are several ways that you can improve ⁴*them / your / it*. Exercises can strengthen your back and shoulders to help you sit and stand taller. Specific stretching exercises can have ⁵*the same / similar results / them*. Posture correctors can also help. ⁶*They / It / Their* are usually worn around the chest and shoulders, holding the back straight and the shoulders back. These days, you can even use an app to improve your posture. Some apps simply send you reminders to take a break to stand up, stretch, and check your posture. ⁷*Some / Them / One* uses a webcam to monitor your posture and tells you to improve it. Apps that use your phone or a sensor attached to your back do ⁸*similar results / it / the same*.

3 GRAMMAR AND VOCABULARY

A **Add another sentence using the cues in parentheses and your own ideas. Do research if necessary.**

1 Taking a walk after a big meal can help your digestion. (do the same)

2 Drinking a lot of water helps improve circulation. (similar results)

3 Some people have a very sedentary lifestyle. (they, their)

4 Sugary sodas are not beneficial to the immune system. (are)

5 People often have bad posture at their desks or when looking at their phones. (this)

A GOOD NIGHT'S SLEEP

1 VOCABULARY: Discussing (lack of) sleep (phrasal verbs)

A   (Circle) the correct word to complete each phrasal verb.

1 add _____	up	out	away
2 rack _____	in	off	up
3 pack something _____ something	into	over	up
4 build _____	into	down	up
5 cut back _____ something	up	into	on
6 cut _____ something	in	out	over
7 drift _____	of	within	off
8 fit something _____ something	up	into	of
9 wind _____	down	over	off
10 drive somebody _____ something	at	to	of
11 slip _____	to	away	from
12 keep somebody _____	at	to	up

B   **Complete the sentences with the correct forms of the phrasal verbs from exercise 1A.**

1   I have so much to do that it's difficult for me to _____*fit*_____ seven or eight hours of sleep _____*into*_____ my day.

2   Reading a book helps me to _____ and relax after a stressful day.

3   I went to bed early last night and actually managed to _____ eight hours of sleep.

4   I'm trying to _____ sugar from my diet, so I don't drink or eat anything with sugar in it.

5   I feel like I just got to work, but I've been here for six hours already. Time just _____ .

6   I tried to stay awake during the movie, but I was so tired that I _____ .

7   If you don't deal with stress right away, it will just _____ and get worse.

8   I have eight meetings today! I don't think I can _____ anything else _____ my day.

9   My neighbor's loud music _____ me _____ all night.

10   You should _____ caffeine. Try to have just one cup of coffee a day.

11   My stressful job _____ me _____ go to the gym every evening. Working out helps me de-stress.

12   I was going to take a short nap, but the minutes _____ to hours and I slept half the day.

2 GRAMMAR: Continuous infinitives

A **Correct the mistakes in the sentences.**

1 He seems to ^*be* spending a lot of time online.

2 You should to be sleeping, not watching movies all night long.

3 For the next two nights, I'm going to be sleep in the living room because I just painted my bedroom.

4 You might to be sleeping badly because there's too much light in your bedroom.

5 I'd like to living in a quieter neighborhood by this time next year.

6 They appear asking people about their sleep habits.

B **Write sentences with continuous infinitives. Use the cues in parentheses.**

1 (teenagers / should / sleep / eight to ten hours a night)

_____

2 (six-year-olds / need / get / ten to eleven hours of sleep each night)

_____

3 (my son / might / not / sleep / enough)

_____

4 (she / appear / stay up / too late every night)

_____

5 (you / could / drink / too much coffee during the day)

_____

6 (the baby / seem / wake up now)

_____

3 GRAMMAR AND VOCABULARY

A **Read the letter from "Not Sleeping" and write a response using continuous infinitives and the cues in parentheses.**

ADVICE FROM MS. WISDOM

Dear Ms. Wisdom,

I'm tired all the time, and I'm not sure what to do. I wake up at 6 a.m. every morning and go to the gym for an hour. Then I take a shower and go to school. I have classes until noon, and then I work from 1:00 to 5:00. I get home at around 5:30 and I have dinner. Then I study for a few hours. At about 10:00, I go to bed and spend a couple of hours looking at social media posts or watching TV. I try to go to sleep around midnight, but I have trouble falling asleep.

So tired,

Not Sleeping

1 (comment on ongoing action with *pack into* and *appear* or *seem*)

_____

2 (comment on intentions or plans with *cut back on* and *need*)

_____

3 (speculate with *keep up* and *could* or *might*)

_____

4 (criticize with *wind down* and *should*)

_____

CLEARING THE AIR

1 LISTENING

A 🔊 **9.01** **LISTEN FOR PURPOSE** Listen to an interview with two candidates for mayor of Barton and answer the questions.

1 Is Karen Green interested in finding solutions to the water quality issues? Yes No
2 Is Michael Lee interested in finding solutions to the water quality issues? Yes No
3 Is the interviewer satisfied with Karen Green's answers? Yes No
4 Is the interviewer satisfied with Michael Lee's answers? Yes No

B 🔊 **9.01** **LISTEN FOR PURPOSE** Listen again and check (✓) the phrases and sentences you hear.

1 Wouldn't you agree that this is an issue that deserves attention? ☐
2 Are you suggesting that … is not an issue? ☐
3 Well, that's certainly an interesting claim, but I'd like to see some facts to back that up. ☐
4 Isn't it fair to say that the situation is critical? ☐
5 I'll have to get back to you on that. ☐
6 Well, that's an interesting point … . ☐
7 Don't you think it's time …? ☐
8 How do you explain the fact that …? ☐
9 How exactly are you proposing to do that …? ☐
10 I'm afraid I can't comment on the issue at the moment. ☐

C 🔊 **9.02** **LISTEN FOR STRESSED AND UNSTRESSED GRAMMAR WORDS** Listen to the sentences from the interview. **Underline** the complex noun phrase in each sentence. (Circle) the word with the main stress.

1 Residents of the city of Barton want clean water.
2 Their fear of drinking contaminated water has driven them to rely on bottled water for drinking and cooking.
3 Several studies illustrating Barton's growing water pollution problem have been published in the local newspaper, Ms. Green.
4 These experts in water pollution and safety will be able to help me design a plan to clean up our water supply.
5 If I am elected mayor, a committee consisting of some of these experts, local engineers, and city employees will take action to make sure that our residents have clean water to drink.

2 CRITICAL THINKING

A **THINK CRITICALLY** What are two possible reasons that one of the mayoral candidates does not give straight answers to the interviewer's questions?

1 _____

2 _____

3 SPEAKING

A **Number the conversation in order.**

_____ **Mayor** Well, that's certainly an interesting claim, but I'd like to see some facts to back that up. I haven't seen any proof that landlords are asking for twice as much money.

_____ **Interviewer** This city is growing fast, and because so many people are looking for apartments, some landlords are charging double the usual rent.

_____ **Interviewer** How do you explain the fact that long-time residents are moving to neighboring cities to find housing?

_____ **Interviewer** Some of these long-time residents are taking their businesses with them when they move. We've already lost ten percent of our local businesses. Are you suggesting that that is not an issue?

_1_ **Interviewer** Don't you think maybe it's a good idea to talk about the housing prices in this city?

_____ **Mayor** I'll need to get back to you on that after I've done some research on local businesses.

_____ **Mayor** I'm glad you brought that up. We certainly are looking into housing prices.

_____ **Mayor** Well, I'm afraid I can't comment on that. It may be that they prefer the other cities.

B **Imagine that a lot of cars are suddenly being stolen in your city. Write an interview with a police officer. The police officer does not know all the details and isn't ready to give straight answers. Use probing questions and phrases to deflect or buy time to think.**

Interviewer _____

Police officer _____

Interviewer _____

Police officer _____

Interviewer _____

Police officer _____

Interviewer _____

Police officer _____

9.4 A THIRSTY WORLD

1 READING

A **IDENTIFY PURPOSE** Read the article. Does the writer seem to have an emotional connection to the story? **Underline** one sentence that supports your answer.

Feeding a Hungry World

World hunger is one of the major challenges we face today. It is estimated that nearly eleven percent of the population is underfed. Although there are almost eight billion people on the planet, and experts predict that there will be more than ten billion by the year 2100, the problem is not with the food supply per se. Globally, we produce more than enough food to feed everyone. However, that food is not getting to hundreds of millions of people around the world.

So what, then, is the cause of the food crisis? The main contributing factor in world hunger is poverty. Nearly one billion people live under the poverty line, meaning they have less than $1.90 to spend a day. Consider that the next time you spend $5 on a cup of coffee. Many people, particularly people in developing countries, simply cannot afford to buy nutritious food. In addition, poverty by its very nature creates more poverty. As a matter of course, poverty leads to hunger and malnutrition, which leads to illness, physical weakness, and mental exhaustion. As such, malnourished people don't have the ability or the energy to work and earn money, so the cycle of poverty continues. Financial donations help, but they can't solve the problem, which, fundamentally, is the lack of regular access to healthy food.

An organization called Groundswell International is attempting to solve the world hunger crisis by providing that access, one community at a time … .

B **Write answers to the questions.**

1 Globally, how many people don't have enough food?

2 How high will the global population get by the year 2100?

3 How many people live under the poverty line?

4 What is the poverty line in dollars per day?

2 CRITICAL THINKING

A **THINK CRITICALLY** Answer the questions.

1 What do you think might be another cause of world hunger?

2 What is one way that you could contribute to a solution to hunger in your own community?

3 WRITING

A (Circle) the correct adverbials to complete the paragraph.

Community, ¹*by definition / as such / per se*, is a group of people who live together in the same place. ²*In and of itself / Per se / As such*, members of a community should help each other. It has come to my attention that many elderly people in this community don't have access to good food. The local food bank has groceries for people in need, but this won't solve the problem ³*by definition / in and of itself / by its very nature*. ⁴*Fundamentally / As a matter of course / As such*, the issue is that the majority of our elderly residents are unable to get to the food bank or the supermarket to get groceries. The majority of them are also unable to prepare food for themselves, so ⁵*by its very nature / at its heart / as a matter of course*, they don't get the nourishment that they need.

B **Groundswell International is an organization that provides people with the resources to produce their own food. Read the information about the organization and write an explanatory paragraph about how it helps solve the world hunger crisis.**

Groundswell International teaches family farmers how to:

- improve and regenerate their soil
- harvest rainwater for farming
- improve their seed supplies

The family farmers are able to:

- grow food for their families and their community
- earn money from farming
- send their children to school

CHECK AND REVIEW

Read the statements. Can you do these things?

UNIT 9	Mark the boxes. ☑ I can do it. ? I am not sure.		If you are not sure, go back to these pages in the Student's Book.
	I can ...		
VOCABULARY	☐ discuss health issues.		page 86
	☐ discuss (lack of) sleep (phrasal verbs).		page 88
GRAMMAR	☐ use referencing techniques.		page 87
	☐ use continuous infinitives.		page 89
LISTENING AND SPEAKING SKILLS	☐ listen for purpose in an interview.		page 90
	☐ ask probing questions, buy time to think, and deflect.		page 91
READING AND WRITING SKILLS	☐ identify purpose in an article.		page 92
	☐ write an explanatory paragraph.		page 93

1 **VOCABULARY: Discussing global food issues**

A   Find the words from the box in the word search.

appetite	cattle	cereal	consumption	fiber
foodstuffs	grain	livestock	nutritious	shortage
superfood	supply	wholesome		

S	P	O	G	R	C	F	O	F	O	O	S	A	F	G	F	O	N	S	E	L	A	G
E	A	N	C	R	A	W	A	B	L	A	D	N	R	S	W	G	F	I	B	E	R	O
S	G	U	T	S	H	O	R	T	A	G	E	C	V	E	R	R	S	B	W	S	I	R
T	A	T	E	W	S	E	O	B	S	A	R	N	F	O	R	A	C	F	K	A	N	G
L	C	R	S	H	I	W	P	A	U	G	I	A	T	T	L	I	U	T	G	A	D	V
F	K	I	B	O	K	C	O	N	S	U	M	P	T	I	O	N	V	X	C	G	B	N
W	S	T	N	L	F	E	D	S	Y	S	U	P	E	R	F	O	O	D	R	S	M	O
G	A	I	V	E	N	O	G	T	A	O	N	E	K	G	O	B	I	H	L	Z	E	U
F	O	O	D	S	T	U	F	F	S	F	W	T	C	O	A	C	E	N	M	O	E	N
D	C	U	L	O	S	U	O	M	U	I	F	I	A	L	I	V	E	S	T	O	C	K
T	U	S	D	M	B	W	O	T	P	C	S	T	E	D	B	N	R	W	A	I	H	L
O	K	V	T	E	C	R	N	G	P	H	C	E	R	E	A	L	O	K	G	Y	R	I
N	R	C	A	T	T	L	E	B	L	C	L	I	S	P	P	N	W	C	A	N	O	P
V	F	B	A	D	M	W	D	X	Y	K	M	L	C	G	I	N	U	C	N	T	N	H
L	P	B	W	S	S	I	H	F	Y	S	A	R	N	R	N	O	L	T	E	M	U	A

B   Write the correct word from exercise 1A next to each definition.

1   farm animals, such as cows, pigs, and chickens _____

2   the process of using or eating something so that it no longer exists _____

3   a seed from a plant, such as wheat _____

4   a food that is thought to be good for your health in many ways _____

5   an amount of something that is available for use _____

6   a lack of something that is wanted or needed _____

7   a desire to eat something _____

8   containing vitamins and minerals and other things your body needs _____

9   anything used as food _____

2 GRAMMAR: Simple past for unreal situations

A **Read the sentences. Write *A* (has already happened) or *W* (the speaker would like to happen).**

1 A company called Beyond Meat created a meat alternative that tastes like meat. ___

2 It's time we all tried different meat alternatives. ___

3 I tried a shrimp alternative made from pea protein and other ingredients. ___

4 Some people would rather we never started raising cows for beef. ___

5 What if someone created a meat alternative that tasted better than beef? ___

6 Imagine if you could create your own meat out of vegetables. ___

B **Rewrite the sentences to use the simple past and the phrases in parentheses.**

1 People should start eating less meat. (It's time)

2 Maybe we can make meat in a laboratory. (What if we)

3 It's urgent that we find a better food source. (It's high time)

4 Picture this—we eat only bugs. (Imagine if)

5 Some people prefer that we find an alternative to eating meat. (would rather)

6 Can you imagine not eating meat for the rest of your life? (Imagine if you)

7 It's urgent that we make changes to protect the environment. (It's high time)

3 GRAMMAR AND VOCABULARY

A **Complete the sentences with the cues in parentheses and your own ideas. Do research if necessary.**

1 Imagine if (supply)

2 What if (grains)

3 Vegetarians would rather (appetite)

4 It's time (consumption)

5 It's high time (superfoods)

10.2 ACCIDENTAL STARTUPS

1 VOCABULARY: Discussing global energy issues

A (Circle) the correct words to complete the sentences.

1 Aspen, Colorado is *low-carbon / powered / biofuel* by 100% clean energy.

2 In places where a lot of people live *off-grid / low-carbon / fossil fuel*, alternative energy sources are their only option.

3 Healthy food, like fruits and vegetables, *renewable / low-carbon / energize* you better than sugary foods do.

4 It's important for people who live off-grid to have *energize / carbon footprint / self-sustainable* energy sources.

5 You can put *solar panels / fossil fuel / biofuel* on your roof and use the sun's energy for electrical devices in your home.

6 Wind power is a(n) *off-grid / carbon-neutral / fossil fuel* source of energy. It doesn't produce any greenhouse gases.

7 Some cars run on *biofuel / fossil fuel / carbon footprint* made from vegetable oil rather than gasoline.

8 Many car companies now offer *renewable / self-sustainable / low-emission* vehicles that run on electricity, or a combination of electricity and gasoline.

9 We need to find *low-carbon / carbon footprint / off-grid* alternatives to gasoline and oil.

10 We can't rely only on *solar panels / fossil fuels / biofuels* because the supply is running out and they are bad for the environment.

11 It's important to try to reduce your *carbon footprint / fossil fuel / power* by using less gasoline and producing less garbage.

12 We need to use *biofuel / off-grid / renewable* energy sources, like the sun and the wind.

B Write the part of speech (*noun*, *verb*, *adjective*, or *adverb*) for each answer in exercise 1B.

1 _____	4 _____	7 _____	10 _____
2 _____	5 _____	8 _____	11 _____
3 _____	6 _____	9 _____	12 _____

2 GRAMMAR: *It* constructions

A **Correct the mistakes in the sentences.**

1 It is believe that solar power can be a source of energy almost anywhere.

2 Is reported that over 100 cities are powered by at least 70% renewable energy.

3 It would seems that these cities have found reliable alternatives to fossil fuels.

4 It would appeared that many other cities are willing to try switching to renewable energy sources.

5 It claim that we will run out of oil by around 2070.

6 It was appear that we need to find an alternative to oil sooner than later.

B **Write sentences with the cues in parentheses.**

1 (it / seem / solar power / one good alternative to fossil fuels)

2 (it / report / we may not / able to rely / on solar energy alone)

3 (it / appear / solar energy / not 100% reliable)

4 (it / believe / best solution / to use multiple sources / renewable energy)

5 (it / hope / we / find / more alternative energy sources)

6 (it / claim / fossil fuels / soon disappear)

3 GRAMMAR AND VOCABULARY

A **Write sentences using the phrase from Column A and the word from Column B. Do research if necessary.**

	Column A	Column B
1	It is believed	renewable
2	It is reported	carbon footprints
3	It would seem	low-emission
4	It would appear	power
5	It is hoped	fossil fuels

1   LISTENING

A   ◀)) **10.01**   **DISTINGUISH MAIN IDEAS FROM DETAILS**   **Look at the topics. Circle the two that you think are main ideas. Then listen to Carla and Max's conversation and check your answers.**

   a   We should produce less garbage.

   b   We should not buy packaged foods.

   c   You can limit yourself to one jar of garbage for the year.

   d   You can buy milk in recyclable glass jars.

   e   We should use less plastic.

   f   You can just recycle your plastic.

   g   A lot of plastic doesn't get recycled.

   h   Plastic hurts marine life.

   i   There is an island of plastic in the ocean.

   j   Energy drinks come in plastic bottles.

   k   Limiting your garbage production makes you think about what you're buying.

   l   Limiting your garbage production makes you eat better.

B   ◀)) **10.01**   **LISTEN FOR DETAILS**   **Listen again. Which points does Carla make and which ones does Max make? Check the correct column.**

	Carla	Max
1 We should produce less garbage.	☐	☐
2 We should not buy packaged foods.	☐	☐
3 You can limit yourself to one jar of garbage for the year.	☐	☐
4 You can buy milk in recyclable glass jars.	☐	☐
5 We should use less plastic.	☐	☐
6 You can just recycle your plastic.	☐	☐
7 A lot of plastic doesn't get recycled.	☐	☐
8 Plastic hurts marine life.	☐	☐
9 There is an island of plastic in the ocean.	☐	☐
10 Energy drinks come in plastic bottles.	☐	☐
11 Limiting your garbage production makes you think about what you're buying.	☐	☐
12 Limiting your garbage production makes you eat better.	☐	☐

2   CRITICAL THINKING

A   **THINK CRITICALLY**   **Why do you think some people are resistant to switching from fossil fuels to renewable energy?**

_____

_____

_____

_____

3 SPEAKING

A Complete the sentences with the phrases from the box.

all I'm saying	as simple as that	comes down to
so much more that	that difficult	point I'm trying to make

1 A lot of people recycle and drive low-emission cars, but there's _____ can be done.

2 You can reduce your plastic waste. I mean, it's not _____ .

3 You can take public transportation instead of driving in order to reduce your carbon footprint, but it's not

_____ .

4 Just try buying fewer foods that are packaged in plastic. That's _____ .

5 It all _____ being aware of your how big your carbon footprint is.

6 We don't need to use plastic bags for our produce. That's the _____ .

B Imagine that your friend is telling you that solar panels are the best way to reduce your carbon footprint. Write a conversation about it and disagree with your friend. Use expressions for defending your opinion and concluding a turn.

Your friend   I think putting solar panels on my house is the best way to reduce my carbon footprint.

You   _____

Your friend   _____

You   _____

Your friend   _____

You   _____

Your friend   _____

10.4 WHAT'S YOURS IS MINE

1 READING

A Before you read, what do you think of peer-to-peer car sharing, in which individuals rent their cars out to people when they're not using them? Circle your answer.

It's a good idea.   It's a bad idea.

B **PREDICT FROM CONTENT** Look at the key words and phrases related to the discussion thread below. Which do you think will be used to defend peer-to-peer car sharing and which will be used to criticize it? Write *D* (defend) or *C* (criticize). Read the thread and check your answers.

1 financial risk ___
2 increased insurance rates ___
3 great alternative ___

4 financial rewards ___
5 subsidize ___
6 acceptable risk ___

Peer-to-Peer Car Sharing—Good or Bad?

With the rise of the sharing economy, anyone can earn money by sharing their knowledge, their homes, and their work spaces. What do you think about peer-to-peer car sharing?

A Joseph

At first glance it would seem that renting out your car when you're not using it is an easy way to make some extra money. However, with respect to the financial aspect of peer-to-peer car sharing, you could be taking a big financial risk. What if the driver gets into an accident? Would you be facing increased insurance rates? Who would be responsible for paying for any damage caused? In brief, I think this kind of car sharing is a bad idea.

B Zarina

Regarding the risks and rewards of peer-to-peer car sharing, I think the financial rewards far outweigh the risks. Car owners can earn more than $10 an hour in some places. Rent your car out for ten hours a week, and you're bringing in an extra $400 a month. By no means am I suggesting that you should participate if you feel uncomfortable doing so. For some, however, it is a great way to subsidize the cost of a car.

C Miguel

It's probably true that there is a certain level of acceptable risk when renting a car out to strangers. From the perspective of a car renter, though, peer-to-peer car sharing is a great alternative to buying a car or renting one from a rental agency. Wouldn't you rather pay a few dollars to rent a car for an hour than pay for a whole day when you don't need it that long?

C **IDENTIFY MAIN POINTS AND OPINION** Read the thread again. Match the contributors to the main points they make. Then circle the names of the contributors who are in favor of peer-to-peer car sharing.

1 Joseph ___
2 Zarina ___
3 Miguel ___

a It's a great way to make extra money.
b It's too big of a financial risk.
c It's a good alternative to renting from an agency.

2 CRITICAL THINKING

A **THINK CRITICALLY** Which of the opinions in the discussion thread do you agree with? Why? Has your opinion changed about the topic? If so, in what way?

80

WRITING

A   Which phrases can complete the sentences? Write the phrases from the box in the correct places in the chart.

by no means	even if you wouldn't	in a nutshell,	in brief,
in terms of	in this respect,	it would seem	not at all
regarding	regardless of whether you would	with respect to	

1 _____ peer-to-peer car sharing
  rewards both car owners and car renters.

2 _____ like to participate, it's a good
  idea in general.

3 _____ accidents, you should make
  sure you have a good insurance plan.

4 Peer-to-peer car sharing is _____ a
  solution for everyone.

B   Write a formal summary of the discussion thread, focusing on the positive viewpoints. Use the expressions in exercise 3A where possible.

CHECK AND REVIEW

Read the statements. Can you do these things?

UNIT 10	Mark the boxes. ✔ I can do it. ? I am not sure. I can …	If you are not sure, go back to these pages in the Student's Book.
VOCABULARY	☐ discuss global food issues. ☐ discuss global energy issues.	page 98 page 100
GRAMMAR	☐ use the simple past to talk about unreal situations. ☐ use *it* constructions.	page 99 page 101
LISTENING AND SPEAKING SKILLS	☐ distinguish main ideas from details in a conversation. ☐ use expressions for defending an opinion and concluding a turn.	page 102 page 103
READING AND WRITING SKILLS	☐ identify opinions and main points in a discussion thread. ☐ write a formal summary of a discussion thread.	page 105 page 105

11.1 THE COLOR COMPANY

1 VOCABULARY: Describing color associations

A **Write each word or phrase in the correct place in the chart.**

bold	capture	conjure up	convey	evoke	imply	muted
neutral	pastel	reflect	resonate with	saturated	transmit	vibrant

Verbs used for color associations	Adjectives that describe colors

B **Write the correct word from exercise 1A next to each definition. You won't use all the words.**

1 bright: _____

2 suggest: _____

3 perfectly represent an idea or feeling: _____

4 used to describe shades like gray, brown, white, black, or beige: _____

5 not bright: _____

6 accurately represent something that is happening: _____

7 completely full of color: _____

2 GRAMMAR: Subject–verb agreement

A **Write *S* (singular verb), *P* (plural verb), or *B* (both) next to each subject.**

1 The company ____
2 Data ____
3 No one ____
4 Criteria ____
5 Physics ____
6 The team ____
7 The employees at Pantone ____
8 Neither ____
9 Everyone ____
10 News ____

B **Use the cues in parentheses to write sentences. Include a pronoun or a possessive adjective where necessary.**

1 (Pantone / have / over 10,000 colors / in / color library)
   Pantone has over 10,000 colors in its color library.

2 (The criteria for choosing a color / include / the feelings it / evoke)
   _____

3 (Either of these two colors / be / a good choice for our logo)
   _____

4 (The news about Pantone's color of the year / be / surprising)
   _____

5 (Everyone / using / the color of the year in / products / right now)
   _____

6 (Neither of these colors / work / because / too muted)
   _____

7 (Right now, the team / working / on choosing a color for next year)
   _____

8 (Pantone employees / be / experts in color theory)
   _____

3 GRAMMAR AND VOCABULARY

A **Pick a color from Column A and a color association verb from Column B. Make sentences with your own ideas.**

Column A	Column B
green	conjure up
blue	capture
red	evoke
yellow	convey
black	reflect

1 _____
2 _____
3 _____
4 _____
5 _____

1 VOCABULARY: Color expressions

A   **Match each expression with its meaning.**

1	caught red-handed	___	**a**	owing money
2	in the red	___	**b**	get permission to do something
3	see red	___	**c**	be good at growing plants
4	cut through red tape	___	**d**	young and inexperienced
5	turn red	___	**e**	get angry
6	green party	___	**f**	be embarrassed
7	have a green thumb	___	**g**	an ecological political group
8	get the green light	___	**h**	deal with a lot of rules quickly and efficiently
9	green / a greenhorn	___	**i**	not feeling well
10	green around the gills	___	**j**	found doing something wrong

B   **Complete the sentences with the phrases in the box.**

got the green light	had to cut through a lot of red tape	got caught red-handed
green	green around the gills	green party
has a green thumb	was seeing red	

1 Are you feeling OK? You look a little _____.

2 James _____ stealing money from the cash register.

3 Michael's garden is amazing. He really _____.

4 I wasn't sure that my boss was going to let us go ahead with our idea, but we
_____ to move forward.

5 Anna was so angry that she _____.

6 Are you sure Ken can handle the project by himself? He's only been here for a few months and he's still pretty
_____.

7 I _____, but I've finally gotten my visa situation sorted out.

8 I usually vote for _____ candidates because I think the environment is
the most important political issue of our time.

2 GRAMMAR: Articles

A **Check (✓) the correct sentences. Then correct the mistakes in the incorrect sentences.**

1 ~~A~~ *The* color green conveys many different ideas. ☐
2 The people who are colorblind can't see certain colors, such as blue, yellow, green, or red. ☐
3 We have to choose a color for our company logo. ☐
4 Do you like the color we selected? ☐
5 Daniel is still greenhorn. He isn't ready to lead a team yet. ☐
6 That's most beautiful color I've ever seen. ☐

B **Circle the correct answers to complete the sentences.**

1 Those flowers are *a / the / no article* same shade of purple as my sweater.
2 Did you know that *a / the / no article* purple is my favorite color?
3 I just read that *a / the / no article* yellow is *a / the / no article* color of both *a / the / no article* happiness and *a / the / no article* fearfulness.
4 I just bought *a / the / no article* yellow car.
5 I think this is *a / the / no article* best paint color for *a / the / no article* dining room. It matches *a / the / no article* carpet in there.
6 What *a / the / no article* feeling does *a / the / no article* color red evoke for you?
7 She has *a / the / no article* hair *a / the / no article* color of chocolate.
8 I can't believe that *a / the / no article* Pantone has so many shades of *a / the / no article* white.

3 GRAMMAR AND VOCABULARY

A **Write sentences using the expressions in parentheses and your own ideas. Be sure to include articles when necessary.**

1 (a green thumb)

2 (turn red)

3 (caught red-handed)

4 (green around the gills)

5 (get the green light)

6 (in the red)

7 (green)

8 (see red)

IT TASTES LIKE GREEN!

1 LISTENING

A 🔊 **11.01** **LISTEN FOR MAIN POINTS** Listen to the class discussion about food and color. What is the topic of the discussion?

a Colorful foods are good for your health.

b Certain colors represent different nutrients contained in foods.

c The color of food can affect whether or not you want to eat it.

B 🔊 **11.01** **LISTEN FOR DETAILS** Listen again. According to the class discussion, what feelings does each color evoke in relation to food? Write notes in the chart.

Topic	Details
Blue	
Red	
Green	
Yellow	
Orange	

2 SPEAKING

A **Match 1–12 with a–l to make complete responses.**

1	Well, the short answer	_c_	a	understand that.	
2	Perhaps I can answer	___	b	by that exactly?	
3	Would you like to	___	c	is yes.	
4	Sorry, I'm not sure I	___	d	Could you rephrase the question, please?	
5	That's a	___	e	I've understood your question.	
6	Well, I've never really	___	f	take this one?	
7	I'm afraid that's not	___	g	have to say …	
8	Sorry, what do you mean	___	h	good question.	
9	I guess I would	___	i	really my area.	
10	I'm glad	___	j	that one.	
11	I'm not sure I understand.	___	k	you asked that.	
12	Sorry, let me just check	___	l	thought about it like that.	

B **Complete the questions and write responses about the reasons that certain colors are used, or not used, for certain products. Use the responses in exercise 2A and your own ideas.**

A Why do you think soda companies _____

_____ ?

B _____

_____

A Why do you think car companies _____

_____ ?

B _____

_____

A Why do you think computer companies _____

_____ ?

B _____

_____

A SENSE OF IDENTITY

1 READING

A **EVALUATE INFORMATION** Read the article and write notes in the chart below.

Soccer team's name	
Soccer team's colors	

OPINIONS: The New Soccer Team

Our brand-new local soccer team has just chosen its name and colors, and I have to confess that I'm unimpressed by the team's choices. The name the team has chosen is The Dunes, which refers to the sand dunes along the beaches of our town. A lot of locales around town use "the dunes" in their names. For example, our local shopping mall is called "Shops at the Dunes," and there's a hotel by the beach called "The Dunes Inn." I think that the phrase "the dunes" works really well for the mall and the hotel because it conveys the idea of a relaxing beach, but I don't think it's a good name for a sports team. A soccer team should be fast and energetic, and the concept of dunes does not convey speed or energy. Dunes don't move. They just sit there.

The team has chosen the colors blue and brown for their uniforms. These colors represent the ocean and the sand. In my opinion, this is another poor decision. The light and bright shade of blue that was chosen is beautiful, but it evokes feelings of peace rather than energy. The light brown shade that is used in the uniforms doesn't resonate with me at all. It's just a dull, muted color. It doesn't convey energy or speed in any way.

I wish that the team had consulted with city residents before making a final decision about its name and colors. Many people around town are unhappy with the choices. Some, including me, have even written letters to the team, asking them to reconsider their decisions.

2 CRITICAL THINKING

A **THINK CRITICALLY** Think about a famous sports team. What is the team's name? What is its symbol or mascot? What are its colors? What do these things convey to you? Do you think they are good choices?

3 WRITING

A **Read the article in exercise 1A again. Then complete the chart.**

What opinions does the writer offer?	What examples does the writer give to support those opinions?

B **Write an opinion essay on the topic below. Use examples to support your opinion.**

Topic: Imagine that your city is going to have a new baseball team. What colors do you think the team should use? What should the team's name and mascot be?

_____

_____

_____

_____

_____

_____

_____

_____

CHECK AND REVIEW

Read the statements. Can you do these things?

UNIT 11	Mark the boxes. ✔ I can do it. ? I am not sure.		If you are not sure, go back to these pages in the Student's Book.
	I can ...		
VOCABULARY	☐ describe color associations.		page 108
	☐ use color expressions.		page 110
GRAMMAR	☐ use verbs that agree with their subjects.		page 109
	☐ use articles correctly.		page 111
LISTENING AND SPEAKING SKILLS	☐ listen for uncertainty in a discussion.		page 112
	☐ respond to questions for different purposes.		page 113
READING AND WRITING SKILLS	☐ read an article and take notes.		page 115
	☐ write an opinion essay.		page 115

12.1 JOB CHANGE

1 VOCABULARY: Talking about change

A **Match each word with its synonym.**

1	embrace	____	a	change
2	disruption	____	b	adjustment
3	transition	____	c	interrupting
4	implement	____	d	accept
5	disruptive	____	e	a shake-up
6	innovative	____	f	go through
7	innovation	____	g	opposition
8	adaptation	____	h	facilitate
9	resistance	____	i	invention
10	undergo	____	j	inventive

B **Circle the correct word to complete each sentence.**

1 Big changes often face a lot of *disruption / transition / resistance* from people who are uncomfortable with change.

2 My company has been *undergoing / disrupting / innovating* a lot of changes lately, such as new management and a bigger office.

3 Change is often beneficial, but it can be *innovative / adaptable / disruptive* at the beginning.

4 Some people are having a difficult time with the *resistance / shake-up / innovation* to their regular routines.

5 The ability to deal with *resistance / facilitation / transition* is an important quality in this day and age because things change very fast.

6 I really like your ideas for changes to the company, but I'm not sure how we can *disrupt / undergo / implement* them without upsetting our clients.

7 We've come up with some *disruptive / innovative / resistant* strategies to improve our business.

8 I'm finding it difficult to *transition / embrace / facilitation* these changes because I don't agree with many of them.

2 GRAMMAR: The present subjunctive

A **Correct the mistakes in the sentences.**

1 The company insisted that employees are prepared to change offices at any time.

2 The management recommends that each employee becomes familiar with the new plan.

3 The suggestion that we are open to any upcoming changes is a good one.

4 It is crucial that the change goes as smoothly as possible.

5 I ask that everyone works together to implement this change as quickly as possible.

B **Use the words from the box and the cues in parentheses to write sentences with the subjunctive.**

be	happen	listen
take	think	

1 (she / insist / that the team / a break from the project)

_____

2 (I / suggest / that you / ready for anything)

_____

3 (my recommendation / be / that everyone / carefully before making a decision)

_____

4 (it / be / imperative / that the changes / slowly)

_____

5 (they / request / that we / to the whole plan before asking questions)

_____

3 GRAMMAR AND VOCABULARY

A **Imagine that you are giving advice to a friend who is having difficulty dealing with changes at work. Complete each sentence with a word from the box and your own ideas. Use the subjunctive.**

embrace	transition	resistance	disruptive
a shake-up	innovative	implement	adaptation

1 It is crucial that _____

_____.

2 I suggest that _____

_____.

3 My recommendation is that _____

_____.

4 It's important that _____

_____.

5 You can request that _____

_____.

WHAT ON EARTH?

1 **VOCABULARY: Describing change**

A **Find the words from the box.**

abrupt	desired	drastic	fundamental	gradual
lasting	profound	radical	refreshing	subtle
sweeping	unforeseen	welcome		

R	C	A	F	U	T	P	O	I	M	A	E	D	H	U	N	J	F	O	C	F	T	O
X	L	F	P	B	S	K	T	D	G	D	R	J	U	S	A	B	M	M	C	H	I	K
I	E	R	A	D	I	C	A	L	L	U	L	T	H	S	S	U	A	M	V	G	P	L
A	T	O	M	E	D	F	S	P	E	E	C	G	R	A	D	U	A	L	H	Q	M	U
A	K	G	X	S	B	F	R	I	A	J	F	K	Q	B	N	A	P	I	P	O	R	N
U	Q	J	I	I	T	U	L	C	X	R	V	G	C	R	E	T	U	D	D	K	S	T
L	O	D	E	R	O	N	G	O	H	O	U	N	I	U	U	A	N	M	P	H	U	D
S	H	R	C	E	E	D	W	E	L	C	O	M	E	P	R	O	F	O	U	N	D	C
E	R	A	V	D	R	A	S	T	I	C	A	F	U	T	T	T	O	F	I	P	A	F
M	B	I	U	P	M	M	H	P	G	I	U	E	M	G	K	S	R	H	R	A	E	S
T	F	I	U	M	R	E	F	R	E	S	H	I	N	G	P	D	S	O	X	G	M	U
H	E	K	S	D	O	N	H	K	V	T	U	S	C	O	L	E	E	M	U	K	U	B
N	D	X	L	U	U	T	F	U	R	P	I	O	Q	D	O	S	E	T	I	O	D	T
I	A	O	R	I	H	A	E	S	M	E	S	W	E	E	P	I	N	G	F	B	U	L
D	M	S	N	R	P	L	N	P	Q	B	A	X	H	G	P	L	S	J	E	J	B	E
C	I	T	T	X	P	U	D	C	A	E	L	F	L	E	H	I	V	R	A	M	U	P
T	U	A	L	A	S	T	I	N	G	I	N	U	T	O	C	J	U	R	I	V	O	S

B **Cross out the word that doesn't belong.**

1 sweeping   radical   subtle   profound
2 abrupt   sudden   immediate   gradual
3 unforeseen   desired   welcome   refreshing
4 temporary   lasting   continuing   permanent
5 subtle   small   slight   drastic

2 GRAMMAR: Perfect infinitive

A **Complete each sentence with the perfect infinitive form of the verb in parentheses.**

1 The landscape is reported (change) _____ drastically.

2 We were happy (be able) _____ to have a say in the upcoming transition.

3 They might (find) _____ a better solution to the problem.

4 Everyone seems (adjust) _____ to the recent changes.

5 The change is said (occur) _____ abruptly.

6 I could (help) _____ with the transition.

7 Relocating the entire town to another area appears (work) _____ well.

B **Rewrite the sentences to create a sentence with a perfect infinitive.**

1 Someone said that the lake dried up suddenly.
   The lake is said to have dried up suddenly.

2 Everyone survived the changes. They were relieved.
   _____

3 Some of the changes had a negative effect. At least that's how it seems.
   _____

4 Someone reported that a river ran through town in the past.
   _____

5 We were sad because we saw so many people leave the town.
   _____

6 Some people think that the city disappeared under lava.
   _____

3 GRAMMAR AND VOCABULARY

A **Use the words in parentheses and your own ideas to write sentences with the perfect infinitive.**

1 (transition / said) The transition is said to have been gradual.

2 (the move / seems) _____

3 (a drastic change / might) _____

4 (we / shocked) _____

5 (everyone / happy) _____

6 (the residents / sad) _____

"AND THAT'S WHEN IT ALL CHANGED!"

1 LISTENING

A 🔊 **12.01** **LISTEN FOR MAIN POINTS** Listen to Mila and Luke talk about their friend Carrie. Write short answers to the questions.

1 What does Carrie make? _____

2 How did she get into it? _____

3 How has her life changed? _____

4 Is she happy with the change? _____

B 🔊 **12.01** **LISTEN FOR DETAILS** Listen again and read the statements. Write *T* for true or *F* for false. Then rewrite the false statements to make them true.

1 Mila had coffee with Carrie this morning. ____

_____

2 Luke has seen Carrie's handbags. ____

_____

3 Carrie has been selling her handbags to friends for a while. ____

_____

4 Carrie made a bag for her brother's friend, Margo. ____

_____

5 Margo showed the bag to some friends at a party. ____

_____

6 Carrie was very calm when she started receiving handbag orders. ____

_____

7 Margo's Instagram followers have ordered more than 500 handbags. ____

_____

8 Carrie is making the bags by herself. ____

_____

2 CRITICAL THINKING

A **THINK CRITICALLY** What are some reasons that you decide to retell a story that you've heard? When do you choose not to retell a story?

_____

_____

_____

_____

_____

_____

3 SPEAKING

A Complete the expressions with the words from the box. Then write *SD* (skipping details), *RO* (referring to the original), or *SR* (signaling a retelling) next to each expression.

details	exact	rest	speak	story
straight	tell	way	what	words

1 To make a long ___story___ short, …   SD
2 I can't _____ it the way she does.   ___
3 It's much better the _____ she tells it!   ___
4 I got it _____ from the horse's mouth.   ___
5 What were her _____ words?   ___
6 I can't _____ for her, but …   ___
7 In her own _____ , …   ___
8 I don't know all the _____ .   ___
9 And the _____ , as they say, is history.   ___
10 Yes, that's _____ she said.   ___

B Complete the conversations with the expressions in exercise 3A. Several answers may be possible.

1 A That's a funny story.
  B I didn't tell it right, though.
  _____

2 A Are you sure that's what happened?
  B _____

3 A What else did she say?
  B _____ ,
    she's going to try to be a celebrity impersonator.

4 A _____
  B She said, "I have an audition with a celebrity impersonator company."

5 A Oh, wow. Why does she want to be a celebrity impersonator?
  B _____ ,
    she thinks she would "make a great Lady Gaga."

C Think of a story that you've heard recently and imagine that you are retelling it. Complete the sentences with your own ideas.

1 I don't remember all the details, but _____
  _____ .

2 In his/her own words, _____
  _____ .

3 I can't speak for him/her, but _____
  _____ .

4 To make a long story short, _____
  _____ .

1   READING

A   **What is one way that a character can change through the course of a story?**

THREE TYPES OF CHARACTER ARCS

In any story, whether it be told as a movie, a book, or a television series, important characters become different in some way by the end of the story. The process of their change is called a character arc. Character arcs can be broken down into three different categories.

One type of character arc is the transformation arc. With this type of arc, a character essentially becomes a different person by the end of the story. Usually the character starts as an ordinary individual and becomes a hero. An example of this type of character arc is the title character of the *Harry Potter* series. At the beginning of the series, Harry is a normal boy living an insignificant life, and by the end, he is a hero who saves the world from an evil wizard.

Another type of character arc is the growth arc, which as the name implies, involves a character growing in some way. Less extreme than the transformation arc, this arc might see a character become more mature, learn something new, or develop a new understanding. The title character in the movie *Lady Bird* follows this type of arc. At the beginning of the film, Lady Bird seems to hate everything about her life, constantly complaining about and rejecting her hometown and her family, particularly her mother, who is difficult to please. As the movie comes to a close, however, Lady Bird begins to accept, and even appreciate, what she has.

The third type of character arc is the fall arc. A character following this arc makes a series of bad choices, and as a result, destroys his or her life by the end of the story. The character of Voldemort in the *Harry Potter* series is an example of this arc. Resentment over the life he's been given drives him to make bad decisions, which cause him to become less and less human and eventually results in his death.

B   **READ FOR MAIN IDEA**   **According to the writer, what happens in every story?**

C   **ANALYZE CONTENT**   **Complete the chart.**

Types of character arc:	The [1] _transformation_ arc Example character: [2] _____	The growth arc Example character: [5] _____	The [8] _____ arc Example character: Voldemort
At the beginning: At the end:	[3] _he's a normal boy_ [4] _____	[6] _____ [7] _____	[9] _____ [10] _____

2 CRITICAL THINKING

A   THINK CRITICALLY   Think of another movie character that goes through a significant transformation. Who is the character and why does the character change?

3 WRITING

A   **Break this complex sentence into three or more simple sentences. Make any necessary grammatical changes.**

At the beginning of the film, Lady Bird seems to hate everything about her life, constantly complaining about and rejecting her hometown and her family, particularly her mother, who is difficult to please.

B   **In exercise 2A, you wrote about a character from a movie. Now write a review of that movie. Include two or more complex sentences as you explain the plot.**

CHECK AND REVIEW

Read the statements. Can you do these things?

UNIT 12	Mark the boxes. ✔ I can do it. ? I am not sure. I can …	If you are not sure, go back to these pages in the Student's Book.
VOCABULARY	☐ talk about change. ☐ describe change.	page 118 page 120
GRAMMAR	☐ use the present subjunctive. ☐ use the perfect infinitive.	page 119 page 121
LISTENING AND SPEAKING SKILLS	☐ listen for details in a conversation. ☐ tell a story that I heard from someone else.	page 122 page 123
READING AND WRITING SKILLS	☐ analyze the content of an article. ☐ write a movie review.	page 124 page 125

1.5 TIME TO SPEAK Professor Robot?

A   Think of three tasks that you don't like to do and wish a robot could do for you. Complete the chart.

What is the task?	Why don't you like to do it?	How do you think a robot could do it better?

B   Create an advertisement for your robot. In the advertisement, describe what tasks the robot could do and why it could do it better than a human could. Share your ad in the next class.

2.5 TIME TO SPEAK Labeled out

A   Create a survey about brand-name foods (well-known brands) vs. generic brands (usually less expensive versions of well-known brands). Write four questions to ask.

B   Survey your friends and family.

C   Bring your survey results to your next class and present your results.

3.5 TIME TO SPEAK The ripple effect

A   Make a list of effects that you have had on your environment and the people in your life.

B   Choose the three most significant effects and imagine how the world would be different if you hadn't been born.

C   Present your ideas during your next class.

4.5 TIME TO SPEAK Every last detail

A   Choose an event to plan from the box below.

> a class reunion   a team-building weekend for work
> a friend's important birthday party   an evening with clients from out of town
> a weekend-long family reunion   a weekend retreat for artists and writers

B   Think about what you need to do to host the event. Start with big-picture elements. Then list the smaller steps necessary to achieve each goal. Use your ideas to create an action plan.

C   Make a poster to advertise your event. Present your poster in your next class and explain your action plan.

5.5 TIME TO SPEAK Make the case

A   Choose the job that you think is best for you.

> truck driver   park ranger   librarian   software developer
> teacher   sports coach   police officer   newspaper reporter

B   Think about why the job you chose would be best for you.

C   Give a presentation to your class, explaining which job you chose and why that job would be best for you.

6.5 TIME TO SPEAK Planning a surprise

A   Think of friends or family members who deserve a fun, special surprise. Think about what kinds of things they like, what they dislike, whether they like surprises, and whether they have any fears or phobias.

B   Choose the surprise you think a friend or family member would like. Then ask that person whether or not he or she would actually enjoy that surprise.

C   In your next class, describe the surprise you chose, why you chose that surprise, and how your friend or family member react to the idea.

7.5 TIME TO SPEAK Preserving a custom

A   Research one of the following cultural celebrations or use your own idea.

> Día de los Muertos, Mexico   Obon, Japan
> Pchum Ben, Cambodia   Gai Jatra, Nepal

B   Find out about how people observe the celebration that you chose. What rites or rituals do they perform? What kinds of foods do they eat? When does the celebration occur?

C   Give a presentation to your class about what you learned.

8.5 TIME TO SPEAK Make a pitch

A   **Choose one of the services below. You are going to create an investment pitch for it.**

> a restaurant and cooking school where students make all the food
> a company that organizes events to help people make friends
> a hotel where people can stay and take various arts and crafts workshops

B   **Identify the key elements of your pitch:**

- the strengths, aims, and selling points of your service
- questions people might ask
- the problem(s) that your service will solve
- an analogy that will make the idea accessible
- a mission statement

C   **Write your pitch in bullet point format and give a presentation in your next class.**

9.5 TIME TO SPEAK Desert island dilemma

A   **Imagine that you are going to live on an isolated island for two years with one friend. What are three skills that you think you should learn before you go?**

B   **Think about the reasons for your choices.**

C   **Give a presentation in your next class about the three skills that you chose.**

10.5 TIME TO SPEAK Rent-a-Pet

A   **Imagine that you want to start a business in your community. Choose from the ideas below or use your own idea:**

> individuals trade services for handmade goods and vice versa
> people rent out their driveways to people who don't have parking spaces
> people rent out their backyards for parties
> people take turns walking each other's pets
> a community garden that anyone can use

in favor of:

against:

B   **Think of a name for your company and prepare a formal presentation for it. Consider the issues or concerns people may have about your idea.**

C   **Give a presentation in your next class about your idea.**

11.5 TIME TO SPEAK Fly your flag

A   You are responsible for designing new packaging for one of your favorite products. What elements do you need to consider?

_____

_____

_____

_____

B   Choose the three or four most important elements from your list to include in your design. Take notes about the reason for each element and give an example to explain your ideas.

C   Make a drawing of your design.

D   Give a presentation about your new product design in your next class. Bring in the product or a sample of the product to compare to your new design.

12.5 TIME TO SPEAK Every picture tells a story

A   Find a picture online or in a magazine that shows some kind of action and at least two people. You are going to make up a story about it.

B   Decide on the genre of your story and decide who the characters—the people in the picture—are to each other. Then develop the plot and map out your story. Make sure it has a clear beginning, middle, and end, as well as a climax.

C   Bring your picture to your next class and tell your story to your classmates.

The authors and publishers acknowledge the following sources of copyright material and are grateful for the permissions granted. While every effort has been made, it has not always been possible to identify the sources of all the material used, or to trace all copyright holders. If any omissions are brought to our notice, we will be happy to include the appropriate acknowledgments on reprinting & in the next update to the digital edition, as applicable.

Key: U = Unit.

Text
U5: Text about Lullabot. Copyright © Lullabot, Inc. Reproduced with kind permission.

Photographs
All the photographs are sourced from Getty Images.

U1: 3alexd/E+; PhonlamaiPhoto/iStock/Getty Images Plus; Vesnaandjic/ E+; tickcharoen04/iStock/Getty Images Plus; metamorworks/iStock/ Getty Images Plus; Hero Images; Tom Merton/OJO Images; Nazman Mizan/Moment; U2: NicolasMcComber/E+; pixelfit/E+; Ken Redding/ Corbis; Caspar Benson; Sven Hagolani/Corbis; FatCamera/E+; vgajic/ E+; U3: 10'000 Hours/DigitalVision; Ezra Bailey/DigitalVision; Siphotography/iStock/Getty Images Plus; kali9/E+; franckreporter/ iStock/Getty Images Plus; Jack Hollingsworth/Photodisc; wynnter/E+; Bettmann; U4: ConstantinCornel/iStock/Getty Images Plus; Mikko Lepistö/EyeEm; Salah Mrazag/EyeEm; PhotoAlto/Antoine Arraou; RossHelen/iStock/Getty Images Plus; Hero Images; U5: mammuth/ iStock/Getty Images Plus; Matt Walford/Cultura; Vath. Sok/500px; Ariel Skelley/DigitalVision; PeopleImages/E+; Luis Alvarez/DigitalVision; kohei_hara/E+; U6: Spondylolithesis/E+; Henglein and Steets/Cultura; TIMOTHY A. CLARY/AFP; Cavan Images/Cavan; Frank Bienewald/ LightRocket; GlobalStock/E+; U7: hadynyah/E+; Amanda V./EyeEm; Arman Rin, Jr./Moment; fstop123/E+; Claudio de Sat/500px; 10'000 Hours/DigitalVision; Ollie Millington/Getty Images Entertainment; U8: DGLimages/iStock/Getty Images Plus; VLG/iStock/Getty Images Plus; Hill Street Studios/DigitalVision; Willie B. Thomas/DigitalVision; Tim Robberts/DigitalVision; simonkr/E+; U9: pattonmania/iStock/ Getty Images Plus; IPGGutenbergUKLtd/iStock/Getty Images Plus; Hero Images; alex_ugalek/iStock/Getty Images Plus; kvkirillov/iStock/ Getty Images Plus; youngvet/E+; kokouu/iStock/Getty Images Plus; U10: aaaaimages/Moment; SWKrullImaging/iStock/Getty Images Plus; wx-bradwang/E+; Eskay Lim/EyeEm; RusN/iStock/Getty Images Plus; Westend61; U11: kasezo/iStock/Getty Images Plus; scanrail/iStock/Getty Images Plus; Kirk Marsh; fotolinchen/E+; LEONELLO CALVETTI/ SCIENCE PHOTO LIBRARY; CostinT/E+; Thomas Schelagowski/ EyeEm; U12: Thomas Gutschlag/EyeEm; Sam Diephuis; Pixelchrome Inc/DigitalVision; olegkalina/iStock/Getty Images Plus; Michael Tran/ FilmMagic.

The following photographs are sourced from other libraries.

U5: Copyright © Lullabot, Inc.; U6: Copyright © International Olympic Committee.

Front cover photography by Hans Neleman/The Image Bank/Getty Images Plus/Getty Images.

Typeset by emc design ltd.

Audio
Audio production by CityVox, New York.

Corpus
Development of this publication has made use of the Cambridge English Corpus (CEC). The CEC is a multi-billion word collection of contemporary spoken and written English. It includes British English, American English, and other varieties. It also includes the Cambridge Learner Corpus, the world's biggest collection of learner writing, developed in collaboration with Cambridge Assessment. Cambridge University Press uses the CEC to provide evidence about language use that helps to produce better language teaching materials. Our Evolve authors study the Corpus to see how English is really used, and to identify typical learner mistakes. This information informs the authors' selection of vocabulary, grammar items and Student's Book Corpus features such as the Accuracy Check, Register Check, and Insider English.